Problems of Urbanization

Paula Bourne

Canadian Critical Issues Series
OISE Press/The Ontario Institute for Studies in Education

The Ontario Institute for Studies in Education has three prime functions: to conduct programs of graduate study in education, to undertake research in education, and to assist in the implementation of the findings of educational studies. The Institute is a college chartered by an Act of the Ontario Legislature in 1965. It is affiliated with the University of Toronto for graduate studies purposes.

The publications program of the Institute has been established to make available information and materials arising from studies in education, to foster the spirit of critical inquiry, and to provide a forum for the exchange of ideas about education. The opinions expressed should be viewed as those of the contributors.

252 Bloor Street West, Toronto, Ontario M5S 1V6

Canadian Cataloguing in Publication Data

Bourne, Paula, 1941-
Problems of urbanization

(Canadian critical issues series)
Bibliography: p.
ISBN 0-7744-0218-0

1. Urbanization. 2. Urbanization – Canada – Case studies. 3. Cities and towns – Canada – Case Studies. I. Title. II. Series.

HT127.B68 307.7'6'0971 C81-094313-1

ISBN 0-7744-0218-0 Printed in Canada
1 2 3 4 5 TO 48 38 28 18

Contents

Preface

The Canadian Critical Issues Series has grown out of the Canadian Public Issues Project, which was initiated at the Ontario Institute for Studies in Education early in the summer of 1969. The purpose of the project was to stimulate discussion and reflection about controversial issues in contemporary Canadian society by developing a program focussing on these issues through case studies. Since 1969 the staff of the project have collected materials and written cases about contemporary incidents covering a wide range of problem areas. The cases are, for the most part, based on published reports–newspapers, journals, books, legal documents, and government reports. Many of the topical units have been taught experimentally in high schools in Metropolitan Toronto, Timmins, Belleville, Ottawa, and elsewhere in Canada.

The books, adapted from these units, are intended to be both provocative and informative. Case studies are followed by questions and analogy situations designed to stimulate reflection and discussion about the broader issues they raise. Additional factual information is included to bring other perspectives to bear on the cases and the problems they represent. Each book concludes with a selected bibliography of reference and resource materials in print and on film and tape.

John Eisenberg and Paula Bourne
Editors

Author's Preface

The concentration of our population in urban centres raises many issues related to the overall quality of life experienced by city dwellers. Competing claims for urban land and for scarce financial resources are common to all Canadian cities. For example, when the building of a new road, expressway, or public transit facility is proposed, personal needs for efficient transportation are only one consideration. Alternative uses and needs–for housing, industry, recreation, and so on–for the same land and money must be considered. In recent years controversies focussing on such issues have also been characterized by the emergence of various pressure and interest groups, while the rights and responsibilities of elected urban politicians to make decisions have been seriously questioned. At the same time the lack of a clearly defined relationship between politicians at the municipal, provincial, and federal level serves to further complicate the urban decision-making process.

In *Problems of Urbanization* many of the major forces–political, economic, and social–involved in the dynamics of city living are examined in the context of various cases illustrating issues of major concern for urban dwellers. Case studies on urban transportation, urban pollution, and community preservation provide a framework for the consideration of specific and general issues related to the quality of life experienced by city residents. And although all of the cases presented here are set in Metropolitan Toronto, the issues they raise are common to all Canadian cities and, as such, should serve as a catalyst for the discussion of urban problems.

This book would not have been possible without the funds allocated by OISE to the project. I especially wish to acknowledge the support and assistance given by John Main of the OISE Press and David Brison of the Learning Materials Development and Implementation Centre. I also wish to thank Lydia Burton and Rene Salsberg for their editorial assistance and help in finalizing the manuscript. My deep gratitude is extended to John Eisenberg for his support, skilful criticism, and comments. Finally, in addition to the project's secretary, Peggy Bristow, I am especially indebted to my husband, Larry Bourne, whose encouragement and knowledge of the subject matter was invaluable.

Paula Bourne

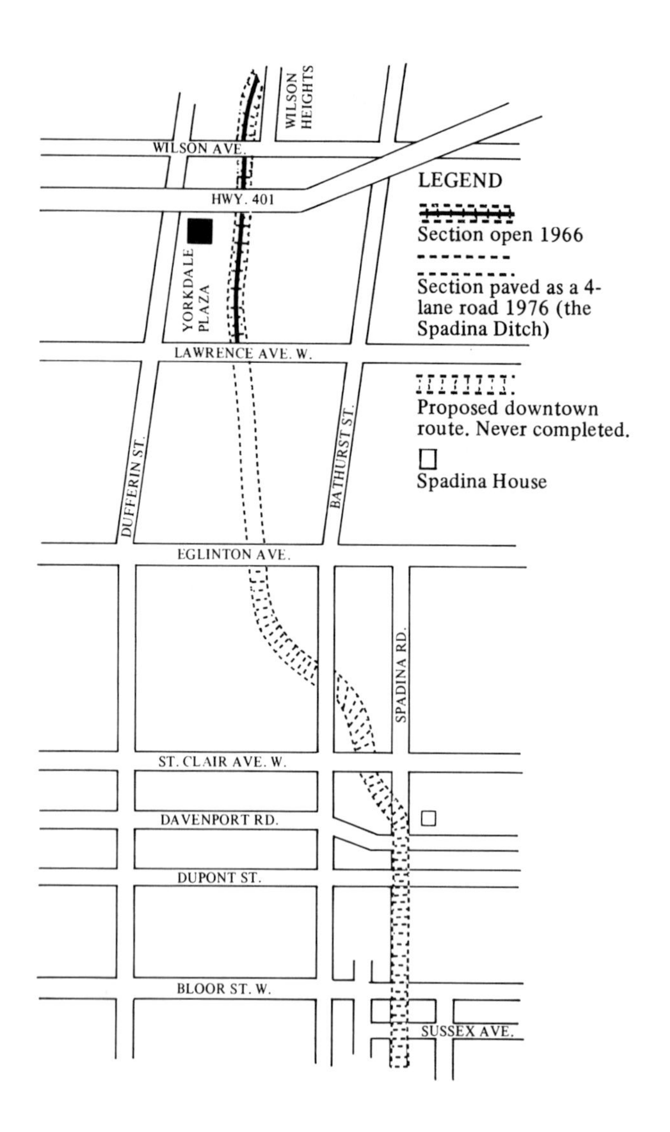
WILSON HEIGHTS
WILSON AVE.
HWY. 401
YORKDALE PLAZA
LAWRENCE AVE. W.
DUFFERIN ST.
BATHURST ST.
EGLINTON AVE.
SPADINA RD.
ST. CLAIR AVE. W.
DAVENPORT RD.
DUPONT ST.
BLOOR ST. W.
SUSSEX AVE.
LEGEND
Section open 1966
Section paved as a 4-lane road 1976 (the Spadina Ditch)
Proposed downtown route. Never completed.
Spadina House

1 URBAN TRANSPORTATION

The Spadina Expressway I

The Original Spadina

In 1819 Dr. William Warren Baldwin built a country home on a hill overlooking the city of Toronto. He named his house "Spadina," from the Indian word "Ishapadenah," meaning a hill or sudden rise of land. Surrounded by a 200-acre [81 hectares] estate, the house provided a spectacular view over Lake Ontario and the sparsely developed area of the city located several miles to the south. A road was built, named Spadina Avenue, connecting the Baldwin estate to the city. It was the widest, grandest street in the area and quickly became the centre of attention for the local population of fewer than 1000.

Spadina Avenue was in the limelight again in 1961 when residents of Metro Toronto hotly debated its future as part of the Spadina Expressway. By that time Spadina Avenue had taken on a much different appearance from the road laid out by Dr. Baldwin; it extended north, far beyond Dr. Baldwin's Spadina house, to form Spadina Road. His original road was located in the midst of an intensely developed commercial and residential area.

Toronto was now the centre of a rapidly growing metropolitan area of approximately 1.5 million people. To accommodate the travel needs of part of this population, municipal authorities approved plans to build an expressway linking Metro's northwest areas with downtown Toronto. Plans for the Spadina Expressway followed the existing route of Spadina Avenue and Spadina Road, both of which were to be expanded and extended as necessary.

The First Spadina Debate

The need for improved transportation between the downtown area and the northwest area of Toronto had originally been debated in the late 1940s. During this post-World War II period new housing subdivisions began springing up outside the city. Because building materials were in short supply at this time and because not all farmers were willing to sell their land to developers, the new subdivisions were scattered along the northern edge of the city and were surrounded by open farmland. These homes were eagerly sought by people wanting to move from cramped city quarters. Prospective buyers, including many war veterans, were attracted not only by modern homes with relatively spacious backyards, but also by the opportunity to live and raise their families in a cleaner environment than was possible in the city. Most of the buyers had lived through the hardships of the depression and the war years, were earning a decent living for the first time in their lives, and were able to buy their own homes. They wanted a higher standard of living than their parents had experienced and living in a new suburban home offered them just this. The "baby boom" of the late 1940s further encouraged the development of new subdivisions as more young families became anxious to move out from the city into a more pleasant suburban environment.

These new developments certainly provided a healthier

place to live for residents than most of them had ever enjoyed, but created a transportation problem. It was still necessary to travel into the city for work, shopping, and recreation since few such facilities were available close to home. All travelling had to be done by car as no public transport was available. Roads were built for driving into and out of the subdivisions, but roads into and out of the city were woefully inadequate to cope with the increased number of cars now using them. This was particularly true of the roads leading from the northwest area of Toronto where a number of subdivisions had been built. Frustrated residents felt that they needed and deserved better transportation facilities. Local politicians agreed and the result was the first demand for a northwest expressway to join these new subdivisions with downtown Toronto. Approval for this expressway had to come from the City of Toronto and the townships of North York and York, through which it would pass. Obtaining this approval proved impossible. While North York, where the subdivisions were located, favored the expressway, the older established communities of York and the City of Toronto were opposed on the grounds that it would cause the destruction of many homes and much parkland.

The Municipality of Metropolitan Toronto and Spadina: 1953-61

In 1953, Metropolitan Toronto was created by the Ontario provincial government. The new municipality, to be known as Metro Toronto, resulted from the amalgamation of the city with its surrounding boroughs or townships. Provincial legislation establishing Metro allowed each of these townships and the city to retain their own elected councils, while it created a Metro Council, consisting of representatives from each individual council. The legislation providing for two tiers of government—one at the city or borough level, the other at the Metro level—also outlined the various responsibilities for each of the local authorities. Responsibility for main roads was given to Metro; local streets remained with the city and boroughs. Among main roads under Metro control were Spadina Avenue and Spadina Road. Metro Council could now plan and approve major new road systems (including the Spadina Expressway) for the Metro area without approval of the city and its surrounding suburbs or boroughs. Thus a better chance for acceptance of a northwest expressway seemed possible.

Between 1953 and 1961 the Planning Board of Metro Toronto together with Metro's Department of Roads submitted to Metro Council a series of plans and recommendations aimed at improving the road system within the Metro area. Route plans for a proposed Spadina extension were included in all these plans. Various bits and pieces of the project were approved and land was bought up in the North York area where the northern extension of the Spadina road would be built.

Throughout these years more and more new subdivisions were being developed. Coordination and planning of these new developments was virtually nonexistent. Developers built wherever they could buy land from farmers willing to sell. Although numerous plans were discussed for improved roads to join up new housing areas with the city, no specific plans were finalized or approved for any, including Spadina. There was general confusion among most Metro residents about whether or not any new roads would be built. Because of the uncertainty surrounding Metro's intentions, there was little public opposition to the tentative plans for the Spadina route. Most people simply believed that the route would never progress beyond this stage. This belief appeared to be well-founded when, in 1956, Metro Council voted to relegate the Spadina to a very low priority position and to concentrate, instead, on extending and expanding other Metro roads where the need seemed more urgent.

The First Spadina Expressway Plans: Support and Opposition

However, while most Metro residents assumed that plans for a Spadina Expressway had been shelved indefinitely, Metro planners continued to work on this project. In December 1961 the planners presented their recommendations to Metro Council members, who approved the construction of one section of the expressway. This one-and-a-half-mile [2.5 km] section was to start just north of the recently completed Metro bypass, Highway 401, and end at Lawrence Avenue. For the route south from Lawrence Avenue into the downtown area, to link up with Spadina Road and Spadina Avenue, the plans were referred back to the Department of Roads Committee for reconsideration.

For many Metro residents the decision to go ahead with the expressway came as a major shock and over the following few months debate on the issue became heated, particularly in letters to the editor published in local papers. At first most of the letter writers were opposed to the expressway because it was too costly and would destroy homes and ruin neighborhoods. Expressway plans to cut through ravines and the large Cedarvale Park were particularly criticized. Such land in the midst of a city was invaluable, it was argued, and if it were lost to an expressway it could never be replaced. Particular concern was expressed about the fate of the Nordheimer Ravine, preserved in its natural state, and providing a total contrast to the densely developed surrounding areas. People wandering through its wooded paths found it hard to believe that they were in the midst of a large city. The expressway would use 250 to 400 feet [76 to 122 m] of the 500-foot-wide [152 m] Nordheimer Ravine and destroy its unique beauty. Many individuals also expressed their fear that if the Spadina was built into the downtown area, Toronto would become another Los Angeles, a city traversed by expressways. Such a move would kill the downtown, turning it into a place for cars rather than people.

However, the tone of the letters published in local papers soon changed, and more and more letters supporting the proposed expressway appeared. The writers argued strongly that the expressway was badly needed to transport people and cars into and out of the downtown area. This apparent change in public opinion—from an anti- to a pro-expressway position—aroused the interest of Ron Haggart, a reporter for the *Toronto Daily Star*. In his column of 26 February 1962, he reported that "suddenly, about the middle of January, the climate of public opinion radically changed. Citizen associations and ratepayer groups, with all the fervor of an Algerian riot, appeared to be lining the streets, urging the reluctant politicians to hurry up with the Spadina highway."

The Yorkdale Connection

Haggart decided to investigate the apparent reversal of public opinion. He discovered that many of the letters supporting the expressway were written by employees and relatives of employees working for a firm called Webb and Knapp. Further investigation showed that Webb and Knapp was a large land-developing company that had a contract with the T. Eaton Co. to build the 25-million-dollar Yorkdale shopping plaza. The plaza, designed to be the largest and most profitable of its kind in Canada at that time, was to be located just to the west of part of the proposed Spadina Expressway. Haggart also discovered that Webb and Knapp's contract was dependent upon "adequate road facilities" for customers to use the plaza. In drawing up the contract, the T. Eaton Co. had defined the necessary facilities as the Spadina Expressway, which would link up the Yorkdale shopping plaza with Highway 401. If the expressway was not built, Eaton's had reserved the right to cancel their 25-million-dollar contract with Webb and

Knapp. Haggart reported his findings to Webb and Knapp officials, all of whom denied that they had encouraged their employees to write letters of support for the expressway to local papers. One official suggested that the employees got together as individuals, wrote letters to the paper, and urged others to do so. "They were worried about their jobs," he explained. "They were concerned that they would be laid off if the Yorkdale project didn't go through."

In addition to his findings concerning Webb and Knapp, Haggart also reported how one North York councillor had organized many of the petitions signed by people supporting the expressway. Briefs from ratepayer associations urging that Spadina be built were also found to have been written by individuals at the councillor's urging. Haggart also noted that many of the ratepayer associations claiming support for the expressway were either inactive or defunct.

The Issues I

Residents' Rights in New and Established Communities

• Given the fact that the new subdivisions in northwest Toronto were approved by the local authority, did not the people who settled there, expecting an improved standard of living for themselves and their families, have the right to be provided with good access to the city?

• Was it the responsibility of the local authority to provide this access? Was it the responsibility of the provincial government to make sure that the residents of these new subdivisions could get to work easily? Was it the responsibility of all the involved local authorities to work together so that good access into the city was provided?

• Did the township of York have the right to stop the

building of a road through its boundaries?

• Do the people living in established neighborhoods in York township have the right to expect that their quality of life will not be disrupted through the construction of an expressway designed to accommodate the travel needs of suburban residents?

• Whose claim do you think is stronger? Why?
  -that of suburban residents for an expressway because by moving to the suburbs they expected a certain quality of life including easy access to and from the city
  or
  -that of the residents of older areas of the city opposed to an expressway because they wished to maintain the quality of life that they currently enjoyed

• Should growth, as represented by the development of new housing subdivisions be (a) stopped, (b) limited, (c) allowed to occur naturally? Why? Why not?

Planning for Growth

• Should the Spadina Expressway have been built when the new housing subdivisions were first constructed to accommodate the needs of a growing population following World War II? Is anyone to blame for this not being done? If so, who?

• Did it make any sense to allow subdivisions to spring up, requiring only minimal approval from the local authority, simply because a developer was able to acquire land for this purpose and there existed a demand for new homes outside of the city?

• Should new suburban developments be planned so that employment, recreational, and entertainment facilities are within easy access for local residents? If such facilities are not planned, should approval for the development be refused?

• Ultimately, should anyone be free to build a home on land that is legally acquired or should governments have the right—indeed, an obligation—to restrict this freedom through legislation aimed at promoting conformity to established planning standards? Would it be right to allow a person to build a small frame cottage in an area occupied by solid middle-class homes?

Analogy
After years of planning, the town of Montor was officially opened in the year 2050. Hailed by urban planners and politicians as the "perfect community," Montor had been specifically designed to provide its residents with all the necessities of modern life. A variety of private and public housing was built for families, single people, and senior citizens. The maintenance of these homes and their surrounding yards and gardens was the responsibility of the local authority. Roads, schools, shops, entertainment, and recreational facilities were also built and maintained by the local authority as were factories, offices, and other places of employment. Jobs were assigned to people by the local authority, and its permission was needed to change jobs. Similar permission had to be obtained by anyone wanting to change houses. People were free to leave the town to live elsewhere but if they did they had to give up their jobs in Montor. In addition to deciding how and where its residents lived and worked, the nature of all local entertainment and recreational activities was also decided by the local authority. The people who chose to live in Montor had to accept this control over their lives. In return, the local authority was responsible for providing a uniform standard of care, including a guaranteed job, for all its residents.

• Is Montor an ideal community? Would it solve the many problems that arise in modern society when new subdivisions are built with little or no planning for the various facilities needed by residents? Is this the best way for ensuring easy access between housing, jobs, recreation, etc.?

- How important is it to you to choose where you will work, live, and play? Is such freedom of choice worth putting up with the problems that result from the development of new housing subdivisions without facilities for employment, entertainment, and recreation?

- Would you prefer to be guaranteed an ordered lifestyle, complete with a secure job, in an efficiently run community even if this meant restricting your individual freedom in a variety of ways?

- Should governments have the right to restrict where people will live, work, and play? If not, do governments have a responsibility to ensure that adequate transportation facilities are provided to meet the various needs of people wherever they live?

- Which, if either, of the following two opposing viewpoints held by urban politicians and planners do you support and why?
  - that before any new housing developments are built, adequate transportation must first be provided to link the new developments with older established parts of the urban area
  - that priority should be (1) building houses and (2) transportation links.

Research Activity

Make a map of the city in which you live and trace on it the distance travelled by your parents and other members of your family to their places of employment. What factors influenced their decision to take their present job? Are suitable jobs not available closer to home? To what extent was your parents' decision to locate in your neighborhood influenced by the nearby availability of employment, recreational, and entertainment facilities? Did other important factors influence their decision? If so, what were they?

The Spadina Expressway II

OMB Approval and Completion of the First Section: 1963-66

While public controversy over the Spadina Expressway raged, Metro Council continued to discuss the project. The provincial government, which was committed to paying 50 percent of the construction cost of the expressway (the other 50 percent was to be borne by Metro), informed the council that they were prepared to construct the interchange at Highway 401 if Metro agreed to complete the expressway from 401 into the downtown area. But although various plans for the proposed route south of Lawrence Avenue were discussed no one route was definitely approved. Despite this lack of firm plans for the completed expressway route, Metro Council on 12 May 1963 agreed to seek provincial approval from the Ontario Municipal Board (OMB) to borrow the $73.6 million needed to build the expressway. Under the Provincial Act establishing Metro in 1953 the OMB was given the power to review municipal spending on projects when the total costs involved would need to be raised over more than "one term of office." In other words, if a project would take more than two years (the term of office for Metro Council) to complete and finance, it had first to be approved by the OMB. Building and financing the Spadina Expressway were obviously going to take more than two years so OMB approval was necessary. The OMB, consisting of three members appointed by the provincial government, met in the summer of 1963 to consider Metro's request. Within a few weeks the board gave unanimous approval, thus allowing Metro to borrow the necessary money to commence expressway construction. Shortly afterwards, work on the first section of the road was begun. Three years later, in 1966, the first stretch of the Spadina Expressway was opened to Lawrence Avenue. At the same time, the interchange connecting Highway 401 to the recently completed Yorkdale shopping plaza was also opened.

Expressway Extension Plans and Cost Escalation: 1966–69

Over the following three years preparations were made to extend the expressway south from Lawrence Avenue. A one-and-a-quarter-mile [2 km] section of roadway to Eglinton Avenue was cleared of homes and readied for paving. From this point the planners proposed running the road via a tunnel south under Cedarvale Park, to prevent the park being destroyed. Because it was far more expensive to put the expressway underground and because of increased construction costs for other parts of the expressway, Metro Council was advised that an additional 23 million dollars would be needed to complete the expressway as planned.

Construction Is Halted September 1969

The escalating construction costs brought the issue of the Spadina Expressway to the public's attention once more. Serious questions concerning the need for such an expensive road were again raised by interested citizens, many of whom suggested that before more money was committed, an in-depth review ought to be made of all Metro's transportation planning needs. Partially because of these concerns Metro Council decided in September 1969 not to seek OMB approval for the additional 23 million dollars and to halt all current work on the expressway until the Metro Planning Board prepared a report on the design, function, and impact of the expressway. These decisions were also influenced by the fact that elections for the city and borough councils were scheduled for early December and it was obvious that the Spadina Expressway would be a major election issue. The planners and politicians hoped that having had a full and open debate on the issue during the election campaign, the newly elected council taking office in January 1970 would have a clear mandate to decide the expressway's future.

Municipal Election: 1969

It was certainly true that the Spadina project was the most central issue in the election campaign. In the city, expressway opponents became organized for the first time, forming the Stop Spadina, Save Our City Committee (SSSOCC). This group was made up primarily of people from the University of Toronto and from the Annex, a residential area located just north of the university campus. Their concern was immediate because if the expressway were to be completed, it would run through the Annex and terminate at the western edge of the campus. Such a route would mean not only the destruction of homes but it would, the SSSOCC argued, increase traffic on local streets and destroy quiet residential roads. While the SSSOCC was requesting an in-depth study of the impact of the expressway, an economic report on the effects of the expressway on Spadina businessmen (prepared at the request of the Spadina Businessmen's Association by a town planner and two university students) was released. The businessmen owned many garment factories and warehouses alongside Spadina Avenue. The report pointed out that building the expressway would force these businesses to relocate in the suburbs. It was estimated that over one billion dollars would be needed to cover moving costs and increased factory and warehouse rentals in the suburbs. In addition, the report noted that most of the garment industry's present employees were recent immigrants who lived nearby and either walked to their jobs or used public transportation. If their jobs were moved to the suburbs, where public transportation was poor or nonexistent, few of them would be able to keep their jobs as they neither owned cars nor knew how to drive. Such a situation, the report concluded, could create a loss of 23 000 jobs for a group of people who would have tremendous difficulties in finding suitable, alternative employment.

Throughout the heated debates over the Spadina issue it was apparent that the project was viewed very differently by residents of the city than by residents of the suburbs. Most suburban residents favored the expressway, to provide fast trips into and out of downtown, and its construction would not disrupt suburban neighborhoods in the same way as city neighborhoods. City neighborhoods are usually old, the houses are close together, and open space for leisure and recreational purposes is limited. Expanding roads or building expressways in such built-up areas causes far more problems than would similar construction in less densely developed suburban areas.

Post-Election Conflict

The opposing attitudes towards expressways held by city and suburban residents became hardened as the election campaign progressed. Consequently, hopes that the city and borough elections would clarify the issues and enable the newly appointed Metro Council to make informed decisions concerning the Spadina Expressway were not realized. When the new Metro Council, made up of 33 representatives from the city and boroughs took office in January 1970, the pro- and anti-Spadina forces continued to argue their cases both within and outside of council chambers. A major concern for everyone was rising construction costs. The pro-Spadina forces wanted construction restarted quickly to avoid even higher costs. Certain city politicians, who had been opposed to the expressway, also felt that it would be "irresponsible" not to complete it now that almost 63 million dollars had been spent. This attitude was not held by many nonpolitical expressway opponents, for whom the fact that so much money had already been spent was no reason for spending even more.

The publication of a book, *The Bad Trip*, summarizing the history of the expressway lent further strength to the "expressways-are-too-expensive" arguments frequently cited by Spadina opponents. The authors, one of whom was a well-known economist, illustrated how the "expensive" Spadina expressway would result in a time-saving for drivers of less than six minutes on an average four-mile trip. This fact was disputed by many potential users of the expressway who saw the Spadina as a means of making their daily commuter trips both considerably faster and more comfortable. No one could convince them that this would not be the case.

Spadina supporters also pointed out that the Spadina Expressway could not and should not be considered in isolation, but rather as one essential part of the 1964 Comprehensive Transportation Plan for the whole Metro area. In 1966 Metro had approved this plan, which outlined the major roads, expressways, and public transportation routes needed to meet the future demands of Metro residents until the 1990s. The stated objective of the transportation plan was to provide fast and efficient travel for all Metro residents. If the Spadina Expressway was not completed, Spadina supporters argued, then it was highly likely that the whole plan would have to be scrapped–resulting in enormous traffic problems for Metro over the coming decades.

These arguments were refuted by expressway opponents who contended that the 1964 plan, based on an outdated philosophy or belief that people preferred suburban living and, therefore, needed fast roads for "personal mobility" was already obsolete. Such a philosophy was no longer true because more and more people were opting to live in the city. At the same time, they asserted, suburban residents were expressing preference for good public transportation facilities, either bus or subway, as substitutes for driving their cars on overcrowded and polluted streets. To many suburban residents these arguments were nonsense. Most of them had no desire to live in the city and for those few who did, city prices for homes were far too high. But whether they lived in the suburbs out of personal preference or not, the majority of suburban residents claimed that they had the right to be provided with fast, efficient roads into the city.

Within Metro Council the question of what forms of transportation would best serve Metro residents' current and future needs became a major topic of debate. At the centre of this debate was the extent to which Metro should commit itself to building expressways and/or new public transportation routes. Most of the city's representatives on Metro Council argued for more emphasis on public transportation. Building expressways, especially into the downtown area would, they argued, result in overcrowding on downtown streets, increased pollution, and a need for parking facilities in areas where vacant land was scarce and expensive. The city requested Metro Council to establish an independent commission to review the 1964 transportation plan so that the full implications of expressway construction could be considered. But this request was turned down by the majority of Metro Council members.

The Metro Planning Board Report: 1970

By March 1970 the Metro Planning Board's report on the design, function, and impact of the Spadina Expressway was completed. This was the report requested by Metro Council in September 1969 when it had halted construction work on the expressway pending the report's outcome. The report was presented to Metro Council along with a recommendation that the Spadina Expressway be completed from Lawrence Avenue south into the downtown area. New design plans for the section running south from Eglinton Avenue were included. The updated construction cost for completing the expressway was now estimated at 142 million dollars. The report also urged that a rapid transit subway line be built, following the same route as the expressway. Space for such a line had been provided for in the centre of the already completed sections of the expressway down to Lawrence Avenue. The cost for the subway line was not included in the 142-million-dollar estimate.

The report answered, at great length, arguments of the anti-Spadina forces. It emphatically stated that expressways reduce rather than increase car pollution, presenting as evidence the results of tests comparing the amount of pollution caused by cars on ordinary streets and on expressways. The reason for considerably more pollution on streets than on expressways was that carbon monoxide pollution does not spread out to areas along expressways, because the steady flow of traffic causes the gas to break up and absorb into the upper atmosphere. By contrast, cars on ordinary streets are constantly stopping and starting, thus producing more carbon monoxide in the immediate vicinity. Another positive effect of steady traffic flow, cited in the report, was lower noise levels than on ordinary streets. Furthermore, the proposed tunnel section of the Spadina was expected to reduce noise level in that area to an absolute minimum.

The report also pointed out that should the Spadina not be completed, it would be necessary to widen a number of residential streets in order to accommodate the travel needs of Metro's rapidly expanding population. This would be costly and would cause more destruction in residential neighborhoods than the construction of one expressway. Referring to the destructive effects of the Spadina Expressway, Wojciech Wronski, the Metro Planning Commissioner, concluded that "the most direct social effect of building the . . . Expressway . . . is the displacement of approximately 697 residential buildings, 44 businesses and one industrial structure." In return for these displacements, the Spadina Expressway would, Wronski claimed, provide a fast, efficient northwest transportation route, eliminate the need for expensive and destructive residential street widening, and reduce noise and air pollution. And these were not the only benefits to be gained by the public, Wronski argued. He produced figures drawn up by Metro Planning Board researchers showing that trucks carrying goods into and out of the city would, by using the expressway route, considerably reduce their travelling time. The researchers estimated that this reduction would result in a saving of three million dollars to the trucking companies, and Wronski suggested that this saving might be passed on to the general public in terms of reduced prices for goods. A final argument used by Wronski in the report to counteract the criticism of the high cost of constructing the expressway was that these costs would be more than offset by the fact that the expressway would attract and encourage office and apartment developments alongside its route. Similar developments had occurred elsewhere when subways and expressways were built, Wronski claimed, resulting in increased tax revenues for the muncipalities in which they were located.

The Issues II

Direct Economic Costs: Whose Responsibility?

- Do you think that the cost of building the Spadina Expressway should be shared as it was by Metro and the provincial government?

- Given the fact that the T. Eaton Company would benefit from the construction of the expressway to link the Yorkdale shopping plaza with Highway 401, should the company have been assessed some part of the building cost involved?

- Should all individual storeowners in the Yorkdale shopping plaza, including the owners of the small ice-cream stalls located there, contribute to the cost of building the expressway?

- Should all businesses located along the route of the Spadina Expressway contribute to its cost?

- Instead of having businesses contribute directly to the cost of construction, should Metro and the provincial government recover part of the cost involved through the imposition of higher real estate and other taxes on those businesses likely to benefit from the expressway's construction?

- Should Metro and the provincial government collect a toll from all drivers using the expressway and put this money towards the cost of building it?

or

- Should all Ontario residents, whether they live in Metro or not and whether they use the expressway or not, contribute through their taxes to the cost of constructing the expressway?

- Do you think that Ontario residents who do not live in the Metro region but who contribute substantially, through their tax money, to the building of all major roads in this area have their interests adequately represented in the provincial legislature? Could you suggest a better way for representing their interests in this respect?

- A large proportion of the money used to finance public education comes from local property taxes. As these taxes increase yearly, many homeowners, especially old-age pensioners and people who do not have children in public schools, object to paying for the provision of a service they do not use.

- -Should people who do not have children in public schools pay property taxes to support public education?
- -If parents send their children to private schools should they still have to pay property taxes to support public schools?
- -What advantages/disadvantages would there be over the present system of financing public education if money for this purpose came from income tax?

• According to what principle should people be expected to contribute to the cost of providing such services as roads, subways, education, welfare, unemployment insurance, and so on.

Economic Costs and Benefits

In the book *The Bad Trip*, the authors claimed that the Spadina Expressway offered little benefit in return for its cost because it would result in a timesaving of only six minutes on an average four-mile trip.

- -Is this timesaving as insignificant as the authors claimed?

  or
- -Is it, as one critic suggested, a significant timesaving when it is multiplied by the hundreds of thousands of trips that would be taken on the expressway?

• In addition to direct costs there are also hidden costs involved in the construction of major roads such as the Spadina Expressway. Listed below are some hidden costs related to the building of Spadina. How serious do you consider each? Why?

- -the loss of parkland in heavily developed areas of the city
- -the destruction of established neighborhoods
- -the destruction of 697 homes, 44 businesses, and

one industry

- the possible loss of jobs resulting from the destruction of these businesses
- the potential loss of 23 000 jobs to immigrants in the Spadina garment industry
- the possible health hazards caused by increased car pollution
- the increased use of scarce energy resources to run cars

• Just as there are hidden costs so there are hidden benefits. Listed below are some hidden benefits related to the building of the Spadina. How important do you consider each? Why?

- the creation of jobs for construction workers building the expressway
- the creation of construction jobs necessitated by the need to replace the homes and businesses destroyed to make way for the expressway
- the creation of construction jobs through the development of high-rise offices and apartments that would, according to the 1970 Metro Planning Board Report, be attracted to locate alongside the Spadina route
- the creation of jobs in the buildings
- the increased supply of apartments made available through the development of new apartment buildings
- the increased tax revenues from the high-rise office and apartment developments
- the possibility of a more vibrant economy resulting from increased employment and increased revenues

• On balance do both the direct and hidden costs involved in building the Spadina Expressway outweigh the direct and hidden benefits?

Research Activity

Using arguments from both sides, write a research paper describing the hidden costs and benefits of building major expressways in urban areas. (*Note*: Suggested information sources include local libraries, newspapers, and the bibliography included in this book.)

The Spadina Expressway III

Public Hearings on the Report: 1970

Reaction to the recommendations and arguments of the Metro Planning Board report were varied–with pro-expressway groups praising it and anti-expressway groups denouncing it. Members of Metro Council did not debate the report immediately after its presentation, but instead arranged a series of public hearings on the report's contents. These hearings were held before the three-man Metro Transportation Committee. Any individual wishing to comment upon the report had to submit a brief (a written copy of his or her arguments) to this committee prior to the opening of the public hearings on 6 April 1970. Over 230 such briefs were filed with the committee, ranging in size from an 86-page submission from a group of ratepayer associations to a one-page brief from a North York resident. People and organizations submitting briefs included students, housewives, pensioners, church groups, and parent–teacher associations. About 99 percent of the briefs received were from expressway opponents. Throughout the hearing's duration, a group of 56 unemployed construction workers demonstrated outside the council chambers carrying placards urging "Build Spadina Now." Their construction union manager described the hearing as a waste of time, and called for a speedy resumption of work on the expressway, claiming that this would provide 400 jobs for his union members.

While the demonstrators paraded outside, inside the council chamber similar arguments to those expressed throughout the Spadina debate were being heard. Expressway opponents repeated their concerns about increased pollution and noise, neighborhood destruction, and increased traffic densities, all of which were seen as inevitable outcomes of expressway completion. The Metro Planning Board report's claims concerning the effect of expressways on atmospheric pollution were labelled as "totally untrue" by Dr. Donald Chant of Pollution Probe (a group of University of Toronto faculty and students concerned about environmental pollution). "The only way to reduce pollution," Dr. Chant told the committee, "is by reducing the number of cars or by putting exhaust devices on cars."

Alderman John Sewell of Toronto City Council attempted to focus the debate away from the potential environmental effects of the expressway. In his brief he concentrated on the financial costs incurred by Metro for building expressways and roads, and compared these to the moneys devoted to other needs. He presented figures showing that Metro was spending seven times as much on roadways as it was on homes for the aged or on housing for the needy. He concluded his presentation by saying: "I question whether those priorities are in order and I would suggest that we have more serious problems than transportation."

In response, Controller Karl Mallette, a member of the Metro Transportation Committee, commented that the Spadina Expressway had to be completed because it was too late to stop it. "Everyone has the right to disagree," he said, "but you don't understand democracy if you don't understand that someone has to make the decision and that's the elected people." His comments, undisputed by other committee members, confirmed a growing suspicion of participants in the hearing that inviting public comment was pointless; that the real decisions would be made by politicians who had already made up their minds to complete the expressway. It was a feeling summarized by Jane Jacobs, a distinguished urbanologist and expressway opponent, when she described the public hearings as a "charade . . . with most of the committee members having already determined their positions."

Metro Council Approves Plans for Expressway Extension
When the month-long hearings were finally over, anti-expressway supporters were demoralized. A week later their spirits were raised briefly when Toronto City Council voted 12 to 10 in favor of requesting the Metro Transportation Committee to order an independent inquiry to decide whether or not to complete the expressway. But the Metro Transportation Committee refused this request. It recommended approval of the designs for the completed expressway as outlined in the Metro Planning Board Report and that tenders be called for construction of parts of the uncompleted sections of the expressway.

On 16 June 1970 both of these recommendations were approved by Metro Council and a deadline of 6 August was set for the construction tenders. No new construction had taken place since September 1969, when all work on the expressway had been halted awaiting the outcome of the Metro Planning Board's report. At that time 63 of the 73 million dollars approved in 1963 by the Ontario Municipal Board for Spadina construction had already been spent. This left 10 million dollars, which Metro officials estimated was sufficient to pay for the paving of the expressway section from Lawrence to Eglinton and the construction of a tunnel through Cedarvale Park. However, no additional construction could be undertaken until the OMB granted Metro permission to borrow the extra moneys needed to complete the expressway into the downtown area. This amounted to approximately 69 million dollars, representing the difference between the 73 million dollars already approved by the OMB and the 142-million-dollar estimated completion cost in the planning board's report.

Within days of the Metro Council decisions, angry letters from anti-expressway supporters appeared in the local press. The decision to proceed with construction in the face of public opposition was strongly criticized. Members of Metro Council were accused of deliberately ignoring the will of the people and undermining the true meaning of democracy. These accusations were hotly denied by Metro Council representatives who had voted in favor of the expressway. There had been, they pointed out, a wide public debate on the issue, with the public having every opportunity to voice its opinion—and only after this had taken place had the issue been resolved according to the democratic process.

In the minds of many Metro residents the issue may have been resolved, but for others the true battle over the expressway was just beginning. An editorial in the *Globe and Mail* summarized the feelings of this latter group when it described the events of the previous few weeks as "the first skirmish." The editorial then continued: "Skirmish? Yes there are some opponents of the expressway who say that we have just heard the preliminary statements of position; nothing more than an overture to the real work . . . Some talk in terms of dramatic confrontations, such as throwing themselves before the bulldozers; others are considering the various legal moves by which the progress of the Spadina might be halted. We would certainly not wish to see the issue die; or to have it assumed that a matter of principle had been settled—namely that expressways (all expressways) are acceptable to Toronto."

The Issues III

The Role of Municipal Authorities

- Should the decision to build the Spadina Expressway

have been made by the elected representatives of all the people living in Metro Toronto, that is by Metro Council? or

• Should each of the three local authorities involved have decided separately on the issue and have had it pass only if there was unanimous agreement?

• Which of these two suggested decision-making procedures do you think would be more appropriate for dealing with the provision of such Metro-wide services as public transportation, sewage systems, and local education? What are the advantages/disadvantages of each procedure?

• During the public hearings on the Spadina Expressway one member of Metro's Transportation Committee commented that "everyone has the right to disagree but you don't understand democracy if you don't understand that someone has to make the decision and that's the elected people." Should a decision, such as whether or not to build the Spadina, be made by council members or is it important enough to warrant the holding of a public referendum in which all Metro residents may vote? Why? Why not?

• According to what principle would you decide which of the following issues should be voted upon in a public referendum? For each one defend your answer with relevant reasons.

- -the introduction of compulsory army service (conscription)
- -the abolition of capital punishment
- -the separation from federation of any province or region

• Do elected politicians ever have a right to take a position they know to be rejected by a majority of their constituents, e.g., the federal government's present position on capital punishment?

The Spadina Expressway IV

Expressway Opponents Seek Political and Legal Support
During the next phase of the anti-expressway battle the opponents decided that, having failed to gain support for their cause at the local or Metro level, they should now direct their attention to a higher level, namely, the provincial government. Throughout the expressway debate members of the provincial government had consistently refused to be drawn into the discussion. It was now time, the anti-expressway supporters argued, that government members took a stand on the issue. After all, they reasoned, the provincial government was involved. The OMB was an agency of the government and with this board resided the ultimate responsibility for deciding Spadina's future. Furthermore, because of the financial cost-sharing arrangements, the government was obliged to pay half the construction cost involved in completing the expressway.

The first attempt to draw the provincial government into the debate took the form of a petition, containing 700 signatures, that was sent to the provincial cabinet requesting an independent review of the Spadina Expressway. Despite a sit-in by members of the Stop Spadina, Save Our City Coordinating Committee (SSSOCCC) at the offices of Municipal Affairs Minister Darcy McKeough, the cabinet refused to act upon the petition. In the meantime anti-expressway supporters were demonstrating outside Eaton's and Simpson's department stores in downtown Toronto. These stores were chosen because both had branches at the Yorkdale Shopping Centre, which the expressway opponents described as being a chief beneficiary of the expressway.

While these activities were occurring, twelve Toronto ratepayer groups were examining various legal procedures to fight their case against the expressway. They learned that under Section 42 of the OMB Act, the board could review and vary or even rescind its previous decisions. Thus the board had the power to reexamine its 1963 decision on the Spadina and could change that decision or reverse it. If the board were convinced that its 1963 decision was a bad one, then Metro would not be allowed to borrow additional money for construction and the expressway could not be completed. After careful consideration of the legal procedures involved, the ratepayer groups decided to hire a lawyer who would then apply on their behalf to the OMB, requesting a review of the 1963 decision to build the Spadina.

On 5 August 1970, J. J. Robinette, one of Canada's leading lawyers, was retained by the ratepayer groups. One of his first acts was to ask Metro Council not to award any construction contracts or to spend any money on the expressway until the OMB responded to his request to review its earlier Spadina decision. In making his request to the OMB, Mr. Robinette cited reasons for seeking the review. These included the large increase since 1963 in the cost of completing the expressway, the increased tax burden this would inflict on Metro residents, and the fact that the most recent design for the completed expressway was "substantially" different from the one previously approved by the OMB in 1963.

OMB Approval Is Sought by Metro Council

Before the OMB replied to Robinette's request for a review, Metro Council members voted in favor of asking the OMB for an immediate public hearing on its application for permission to borrow the money needed to complete Spadina. This move by Metro surprised many people as it had been assumed that Metro would not seek such a hearing until it had spent the 10 million dollars it still had left for construction. The decision to request OMB approval at this stage rather than a later one was also accompanied by an announcement that Metro would not award any further construction tenders. According to Metro Council Chairman Ab Campbell, the council members had decided to proceed this way because they wanted "unsatisfied citizen opponents of the expressway to get the final independent hearing for which they have been asking."

The OMB hearing opened on 16 September 1970. The board consisted of three members appointed by the provincial government; the chairman of this group, J. A. Kennedy, had also chaired the 1963 hearing on the expressway. Because of the increased debate surrounding the issue that had occurred over the intervening years, Mr. Kennedy was aware that the 1970 hearing would be far more controversial than the previous one. In an attempt to set the terms of reference for the hearing, he asked the lawyers from both Metro and the ratepayer groups to submit written statements to the board clearly setting out their reasons for seeking the OMB hearing.

Metro submitted an eleven-page statement in which it requested OMB approval for both completing the expressway into the downtown area and borrowing the necessary money to do so. According to Metro's statement, the only consideration of concern to the OMB in making its decision should be the ability of Metro taxpayers to pay the costs involved. Mr. Robinette's statement, on behalf of the ratepayer groups, argued that the OMB should conduct a complete and thorough inquiry on the expressway question and review its earlier decision on the project. He pointed out that provincial legislation empowered and instructed the OMB to approve public works, such as expressways, only when they appeared to be "necessary and expedient." And according to Robinette, building the Spadina Expressway was neither "necessary" nor "expedient" at this time. To justify this claim, Robinette set forth a number of arguments summarizing anti-expressway opinion.

The OMB's Independent Spadina Inquiry: 1971

When both statements had been received, the OMB decided that an independent inquiry into the whole Spadina project would be held and that the public would be allowed to attend and present any relevant information. This inquiry opened on 4 January 1971 and there followed sixteen days of hearings during which 100 people testified for and against the Spadina project. Both sides to the dispute relied heavily on the testimony of technical experts to support their cases. Metro's lawyer, A. P. G. Joy, had air-pollution experts testify that the expressway would not produce high or dangerous pollution levels. To counteract this evidence, Mr. Robinette brought in a New York air-pollution expert who predicted that the carbon monoxide from car exhausts using the expressway would be strong enough to cause "adverse health affects" to people living alongside its route.

Metro Planners were asked for figures illustrating the tremendous population growth in Metro's northwest area over the past ten years. Similar figures showing an increase in motor vehicle registration were also produced. Wojciech Wronski, Metro's planning commissioner, was asked to comment on the implications of these figures. He described the daily traffic chaos on the existing, overloaded local road system. Quiet residential neighborhood roads were overrun by cars and parents were afraid to allow their children to play outside their own homes because of the high risk of accidents. People needed their cars, he argued, to travel to and from their places of work and entertainment. No one had the right to ban the use of cars, so if people wished to drive, Metro had an obligation to provide, good, safe roads. And, he concluded, Metro residents needed the Spadina Expressway to accommodate their present and future needs. In response to this question of "need" Mr. Robinette submitted a report, prepared by a group of consultants, showing that by 1995 many more people would be both living and working in all of the Metro suburbs. According to the report's writers this would mean less demand for a downtown expressway like the Spadina and more demand for improved road and public transit services between points in the suburbs. Rather than spending large sums of money on any expressway, the report suggested that Metro concentrate its efforts on improving roads within and between suburbs, and on building rapid transit facilities such as subway lines from the suburbs into the downtown area.

Not all of the evidence heard by the OMB during the hearings came from the experts. "The only expertise I have in regard to the Expressway," said one expressway opponent who lived close to the proposed end of the expressway, "is that I'll have to look at it and pay for it." Other citizens, who wanted the expressway completed to ease their trips to and from the city, urged immediate resumption of construction to avoid further increases in cost that would inevitably result from a long delay. On the question of cost, a number of anti-expressway supporters told the board that they considered it immoral to force taxpayers to pay for an expressway when its need had not been satisfactorily established. For some individuals, financial concerns were more immediate and personal. One woman, whose house would be torn down if the expressway was completed, told the board that the amount of compensation she would receive for her home would not be enough to buy an equivalent house elsewhere in the city. "We've been told that you can't force people to leave their cars at home and take rapid transit," she said bitterly. "Yet the man who's telling me that is also telling me to get out of my house and to let him have his expressway so he can drive downtown."

The OMB Decision

After the public hearings were completed, OMB members

spent three weeks reviewing the evidence and preparing their reports. Each member was responsible for his own report and decision. When the reports were made public it was discovered that the board members had voted two to one in favor of Metro's completing the expressway and borrowing the additional money to do so. The approval was conditional upon Metro's having the Spadina subway line in operation before the expressway was completed; Metro officials were also ordered to give the OMB construction and financial reports every six months. The two members who voted in favor of completion were William Shubb and Robert McGuire. Board Chairman J. A. Kennedy dissented and called for further studies to explore several unanswered questions. The split decision was unprecedented in the history of the OMB; prior to 1969 any board disagreement would have been resolved by the board chairman's decision. But under a 1969 amendment to the OMB Act, the majority decision of the board members became the final one.

The Majority Decision

Both of the majority reports submitted by Mr. Shubb and Mr. McGuire stressed the immediate rather than the long-term need of suburban residents for the expressway. "Any suggestion of delay, awaiting further reports," wrote Mr. Shubb, "might very well be fruitless and costly . . . and would be punitive to those who rightfully expect and deserve this kind of facility." "This transportation facility will," said Mr. McGuire, "meet the present needs of the community." He and Mr. Shubb both rejected testimony that air pollution might increase along the expressway route, and accepted evidence that pollution would be controlled. Although admitting that there would be "adverse social and environmental impact" on areas through which the expressway ran, Mr. McGuire stated that ". . . the advantages that will accrue to the greater community will outweigh the disadvantages to those in its path or proximity." Mr. McGuire also commented on the opposition of citizens to the project. "The right [of citizens] to advise cannot be interpreted as the right to supplant the decision-making body [Metro Council] as the recognized political formation in our society, or otherwise chaos would result, and the best motivated persons should not want that to occur."

The Minority Decision

In his minority report, Mr. Kennedy made it clear that his decision was not an outright rejection of the expressway project, but was instead a call for more studies and a comprehensive transportation review, which would allow a more informed decision to be made at a later date. His comments reflected the fears and concerns of many city residents that the potential impact of the expressway had not received sufficient attention. He wanted further study of the effects of the expressway on parkland and ravines, on neighborhoods, and on the environment in general. Kennedy admitted in his report that similar concerns were present in 1963 when he had approved the Spadina project but, he said, at that time they were not strongly felt. The changes in public opinion concerning the expressway were, in Kennedy's opinion, sufficient reason for not supporting the project "without further study."

Mr. Kennedy also urged that studies be undertaken comparing costs of subways, public transit, and expressways in order to determine the most efficient and economical method of transportation. Such studies were, in his estimation, particularly important in a large metropolitan area with increasing population and limited financial resources. Referring to the right of any individual to choose how he or she will travel, Kennedy commented that "machines are made to serve men, not man to serve machines, regardless of whether the machine is an automobile or a computer. Surely democracy (freedom of choice in how to travel) does not dictate that an expressway must be cut through quiet development in a city if that expressway will not solve the problem, especially if another solution can be found."

The OMB Decision Is Appealed to the Provincial Cabinet
Most Metro officials were delighted with the OMB's majority decision, and Metro chairman Ab Campbell lost no time in announcing that, after the seventeen-month delay, construction on the expressway could be resumed immediately. According to Mr. Campbell this would provide 300 jobs for unemployed construction workers. In the meantime, despondent anti-expressway supporters were conferring with legal experts to examine courses of action open to them now that they had lost their case with the OMB. They agreed unanimously to keep fighting and to appeal the OMB decision. After examining various alternatives they decided to appeal to the provincial cabinet. Under provincial law any decision made by the OMB could be appealed to the cabinet. The cabinet then had the power to confirm the original decision, reject it, amend or vary it in any way, or order the board to hold a new hearing. The anti-Spadina groups called on J. J. Robinette to prepare their appeal, which was subsequently submitted to the cabinet at the end of February 1971. Once the appeal was before the cabinet, Metro officials agreed not to resume construction work pending the cabinet's decision.

As no time was set for the cabinet decision and all discussions concerning the issue were limited to cabinet members, the following months were extremely anxious ones for the pro- and anti-expressway supporters. Both groups tried to exert indirect influence on cabinet thinking by maintaining a steady stream of letters to the editors of local newspapers and by speaking to individual cabinet members. The anti-Spadina forces also used this waiting period to organize fund-raising activities to help pay for their estimated legal costs of $40 000. They solicited donations from groups and private individuals, held dances and dinners, and sold thousands of "Stop Spadina" buttons.

The Issues IV

The Role of the OMB

• Do you think that a provincial government agency, such as the OMB, should have the authority to approve or disapprove of municipal projects that require major financial expenditures and/or zoning changes? Why? Why not?

• In a conflict situation where the OMB overrides a decision of a local authority, on the basis of what principle should it do so?

• Should all decisions made by the OMB need the approval of

- -a simple majority of its members?
- -all members?
- -the chairman alone if there is a split decision?

• The role of the OMB in reviewing municipal projects has been severely criticized by local politicians in recent years. Some critics claim that it takes too long for the board to approve major projects and that this results in increased costs for such projects. In some cases, the cost of providing much needed housing has almost doubled because of the need to obtain OMB approval. Other critics argue that local authorities should make their own decisions on all major projects in their areas, and not have them reviewed by a non-elected body such as the OMB.

- -Does increased cost caused by delays in obtaining OMB approval for large projects warrant (a) abolishing the board, (b) streamlining the board's operations

and requiring it to make a decision on all issues referred to it within 30 days?
- In a society that has grown as ours has in the last 30 years, is it not necessary to have an agency, such as the OMB, to act as a watchdog and review large projects requiring major expenditures and zoning changes?

Research Activity
Contact your local authority to see if it has any large projects currently before the OMB for approval. What are they and why is such approval necessary? How long have they been awaiting approval? Has the need for approval caused any increase in the original estimated cost? If so, what are likely to be the implications of this increase? (Similar government agencies such as the OMB in Ontario exist in other provinces. Students living outside of Ontario can contact their local authority to find out who is responsible for reviewing major projects in their area.)

The Spadina Expressway V

The Cabinet Decision: 1971
Throughout the ten weeks that the future of the Spadina was being debated by provincial cabinet members, numerous rumors circulated as to what their final decision would be—that the appeal would be rejected totally, that the cabinet would submit a revised design for the expressway, that the cabinet would call for additional studies on the issue. Although pressed to do so, cabinet members consistently refused comment upon any of these rumors. Consequently, when Premier William Davis stood up in the legislature on 3 June 1971 and announced that the cabinet had reached its decision, the legislative members, as well as the ordinary public, did not know

what to expect. Everyone was clearly surprised when Premier Davis began his statement by announcing that the cabinet had upheld the anti-Spadina appeal and the expressway would therefore be stopped at Lawrence Avenue. The decision was greeted by wild cheers from some legislative members and by loud boos from others. When the commotion died down, Premier Davis continued with his statement. While the expressway would not be completed, he said, the cabinet did want the northwest subway line to be built as soon as possible. No decision as to the route for this line had been made by the cabinet, but Premier Davis offered to arrange a meeting between Metro officials and government representatives to work out details. As an indication of his government's support for rapid transit facilities, Premier Davis added that provincial grants for subway construction would be immediately doubled from 25 to 50 percent.

Having presented the cabinet's decision, which he called a "tough" and "agonizing" one to make, Premier Davis then described some of the cabinet's deliberations on the issue. There had been, he admitted, considerable disagreement between cabinet members and "a great deal of give and take" had been necessary in reaching the decision. The final decision did have the "complete support" of all cabinet members. They were all aware, the premier said, that large amounts of money and time had been invested in the Spadina project, but, in his opinion and that of his colleagues, stopping the Spadina was justified because the expressway represented a transportation system emphasizing cars rather than people. "If we are building a transportation system to serve the automobile," he stated, "the Spadina Expressway would be a good place to start. But if we are building a transportation system to serve people the Spadina Expressway is a good place to stop." His government's decision was, he asserted, a historic one, because it rejected the commonly held notion that in city planning, priority must be given to the rapid movement of cars even though this meant sacrificing homes and parkland. The premier concluded his remarks by reemphasizing his government's pledge to serve people ahead of things. "This Government cannot help but heed the rising public anxiety and concern in questions relating to pollution and environmental concern. I trust that our decision will give further assurance of our determination to respond to those concerns."

Pro and Anti Reaction to the Stop Spadina Decision

Outside the legislature the premier was mobbed by newspaper, radio, and TV reporters all seeking further details of the cabinet decision. The premier had little to add to the remarks he had already made except to stress that the Spadina decision was "final" and that no appeal against this decision would be allowed. Newspaper editorials both praising and criticizing this final decision appeared in local papers the day following the announcement. The *Globe and Mail* praised the government for acting from a concern to do the right thing and making a "courageous decision" that would probably lose them votes in the next election. The *Toronto Star*, in its editorial, praised the government's decision to increase grants for subway construction but was unenthusiastic about the decision to stop Spadina. The issue was not, the editorial pointed out, one of cars versus people, as was suggested by Premier Davis, but was instead one of people versus people: "People downtown who feared [that] Spadina and subsequent expressways would ruin the central city, against people in the fast growing northwest sector of Metro who now lack an efficient means of getting to and from downtown, as well as people who are plagued by heavy traffic along [their] streets." Stopping the Spadina, the editorial stated, would not stop or reduce the number of cars travelling into and out of the downtown section even after the subway was built.

The Star editorial also focussed upon an additional issue arising from the cabinet's decision, namely, that of the proper relationship between the province and the municipalities. It expressed concern for the maintenance of Metro's autonomy and that of other municipalities, if decisions of elected municipal officials were to be overruled by the provincial government as they had been in this case. Various Metro politicians lost no time in pointing out this potential implication of the cabinet's action. Metro chairman Ab Campbell called the cabinet decision "a challenge of the right of elected municipalities to make decisions and plan for the community." North York controller Irving Paisley described the decision as posing a "dangerous threat" to Metro's ability to govern itself. "They [the cabinet] might as well take over the whole council and disband the elected officials," he suggested angrily.

The threat to Metro's autonomy was a major focus for the first meeting of Metro Council after the cabinet's decision was made public. In the general anger over the decision and its implications, some Metro Council members recommended that Metro take legal action against the province requiring it to return to Metro the money already spent on the completed portion of the expressway. It was argued that the 1963 OMB decision represented a joint commitment by the province and Metro to build the Spadina Expressway, and that, therefore, the cabinet decision to stop the expressway constituted a breach of contract. This legal argument in favor of suing the province was not acceptable to all council members. However, there was unanimous agreement that the province did have a moral obligation to reimburse Metro and its taxpayers for the large sums of money spent on the expressway project since 1963. Metro Council did in fact seek independent legal advice on the question of suing the province but was advised against such action.

The legal consultant retained by Metro advised that because the cabinet was acting within its powers when it stopped the expressway neither the cabinet members nor the government could be held liable for any damages resulting from that decision.

While the elected officials debated the implications of the cabinet decision, and the legal and moral obligations of the province, Metro's taxpaying citizens were alternatively labelling the decision "fantastic" or "disastrous." Colin Vaughan, an active organizer of the anti-expressway groups, described the cabinet's actions as signifying "a new era in urban environment and preserving downtown neighborhoods." Another spokesman for the anti-Spadina supporters, noting that it had been ordinary citizens and not elected officials who had organized the opposition to Spadina, commented that the final decision was "an incredible victory for the people of Toronto. . . . The Spadina movement created a base of people power and from this victory there cannot help but grow a link between the people and the elected officials. Elected officials will become aware of the fact that they are to serve the people and that the people's needs must be met."

The Spadina Ditch

The fact that downtown neighborhoods would be preserved and that "people power" had been victorious was no consolation for the pro-expressway supporters. Angered and despondent as a result of the cabinet decision, they asserted that the unfinished expressway was a total waste of taxpayers' money. The two-mile [3.2 km] completed section, going from "nowhere to nowhere" was, in their opinion, useless, because unless Spadina was completed as planned, it provided little relief for the traffic problems of Metro's northwest area. Residents of homes backing onto the one-and-a-quarter-mile [2 km] uncompleted section of the expressway from Lawrence to Eglinton were especially incensed over the decision. Construction work on this section had been completed in 1969 but Metro had delayed paving it when all work on the expressway was halted in September. The local residents, who had suffered through construction noise and dirt while this section was being built, angrily claimed that the value of their homes had dropped as no one wanted to buy a house backing onto an open ditch. They realized that completing the expressway would not solve the problems of noise and lowered property values, but it would improve their current situation. "Now that they've done the damage," said one homeowner, "why not finish it and at least clean up the mess."

The future of this unpaved section of the expressway soon became a major focus of attention. To the anti-Spadina supporters it was symbolic of their victory in stopping the southward extension of the expressway; to the pro-Spadina supporters, the unpaved section—or "Davis ditch" as it was labelled—was symbolic of the stupidity of the cabinet decision. Suggested uses for the Davis ditch ranged from turning it into a park to building houses and apartment buildings on it. One less serious suggestion was that it be used as a burial ground for those Metro officials who had promoted the expressway. Soon after announcing the cabinet's decision, Premier William Davis did approach Buckminster Fuller, an internationally known U.S. housing and transportation expert, and asked him to design a residential and commercial development for the site. In October 1971, Premier Davis unveiled the Fuller design for a $75 million development project that would include shops, offices, and residential units for 12 000 people. Premier Davis's enthusiasm for the project was quickly dampened by the negative reactions of most Metro politicians. Besides objecting to the cost of such a project, the politicians criticized it for failing to solve the traffic problem in Metro's northwest area. Such a project would add to that problem because existing streets would be forced to accommodate considerably more traffic coming into and out of the proposed development project. Amidst these criticisms, Premier Davis did not pursue the project. Although no official announcement was ever made, the development plans were quietly shelved.

The Issues V

The Role of the Provincial Government

• Was the cabinet justified in vetoing the Spadina Expressway when its construction had been approved by Metro Council and a majority of the OMB members?

• Does the fact that the provincial government was paying part of the cost for building the expressway give the cabinet the right to stop its construction? Even if the government did not contribute, would it not have the right to regulate and coordinate all large-scale building projects in the province?

• In what way(s) did the cabinet's decision threaten the authority of Metro Toronto and other local municipalities in Metro?

• Did the provincial government have a moral obligation to repay Metro taxpayers the large sums of money spent on the expressway since 1963?

The Spadina Expressway VI

The Spadina Subway Route Is Approved: 1971

A few weeks after the Buckminster Fuller plans for the "Davis ditch" were unveiled, a joint Metro-Provincial Committee announced agreement on a route for the Spadina subway. This committee had been set up by Premier Davis when he announced that the expressway would be stopped. Its terms of reference were to examine the various possible subway routes and to decide upon the best one. Of primary concern was the route south from Lawrence Avenue, as space for a future subway route had already been provided in the two-mile [3.2 km] completed section of the expressway. A number of alternative southern routes were considered and the one that was finally recommended followed the original plan for the expressway. This meant that the subway would run through the Davis ditch and through the ravine land of Cedarvale Park, the same park that had been the focus for considerable anti-Spadina sentiment throughout the long debate. And once again conservationists objected on the grounds that such a route would ruin the ravine and the park. Premier Davis and his colleagues were assured, however, that the route would result in minimal damage to the park because the subway would be located in a tunnel underneath the ravine. Consequently, the provincial government approved the Spadina subway route, and when similar approval was granted by Metro Council, the necessary construction work was begun.

Completion of the Spadina Expressway Is Sought

Throughout the months following the decision to stop the expressway, while the fate of the Davis ditch and the route for the Spadina subway were being discussed, it was also obvious that many Metro politicians and ordinary citizens still hoped that the expressway would be completed. Whenever the opportunity presented itself Metro politicians were reported in newspapers, on TV, and on radio urging the cabinet to reconsider its decision. Lending considerable weight and credibility to the politicians' arguments for completing the Spadina was a group of citizens calling themselves "The Citizens Committee for the Completion of the Spadina." This committee was made up primarily of residents located in the Lawrence Avenue area close to the end of the completed expressway section. For these people the reality of the Spadina decision was to be seen every day in the constant stream of traffic pouring through their streets en route to or from the expressway's entrance and exit ramps. It was a situation they had lived with ever since the two-mile [3.2 km] section of expressway had been opened. They had complained to their local officials many times, but they had been assured that once the expressway was extended southwards, the problem would disappear. Cars, headed north and south, would then no longer be forced to use their local streets as the only routes to and from the expressway. They looked forward to the time when these local streets would once again be free of traffic, noise, and pollution and would become safe places for their children to play. With the decision to stop Spadina at Lawrence, their hopes were dashed and overnight what had been a temporary problem became a permanent one.

Determined to bring their plight to the public's attention, the citizens committee tried to persuade the authorities to have the expressway extended southwards and away from their neighborhood. Leading their efforts was Esther Shiner, a mother of four children, and a resident of a street located near the completed section of Spadina. According to Mrs. Shiner, there were thousands of motorists using her street alone because the expressway stopped and started at Lawrence. Mrs. Shiner and the committee members organized many protest meetings and sent numerous petitions to the provincial government urging that the Spadina decision be reversed. During morning and evening rush hours they also blockaded the entrance and exit ramps to the expressway with people waving signs proclaiming "Go Spadina" and handing out pro-Spadina literature to the frustrated motorists sitting in the traffic jams. Their efforts resulted in a special traffic plan being devised and approved for the area by the local council. Under this plan a number of the streets became one-way and entrance into and out of certain streets was prohibited during the morning and evening rush hour periods. Although this provided some relief for the residents, it did little to reduce the number of cars entering and leaving the expressway, and was generally regarded as a temporary solution. The only permanent solution to the problem, in the committee's opinion, was to complete the expressway.

Establishing Metro's Transportation Needs: 1972-75

By mid-1972, the Citizens Committee for the Completion of Spadina, together with other Metro residents and politicians who were equally keen to have the Spadina decision reversed, began directing their attention to the Joint Technical Transportation Committee. This committee consisted of representatives from Metro Council, the provincial government's Ministry of Transport and Communications, and the Toronto Transit Commission, whose responsibility included all forms of public transit in the Metro area. The committee had been established by Metro Council in late 1971 and charged with reviewing Metro's existing transportation policies which would, in turn, lead to a revised transportation plan for the Metro area. The Metro Transportation Plan, approved in 1966, had called for an integrated system of roads, expressway, and public transit facilities to serve Metro's transportation needs through to the 1990s. However, after the Spadina was stopped, not only was one essential link in the plan lost, but the future of other planned expressways was also in doubt. The argument used by the provincial government for stopping Spadina, namely that priority must be given to people ahead of cars, suggested to many Metro officials that the government was almost certain to veto plans for any new or extended expressways within Metro. Therefore, because of the Spadina decision and its implications, Metro needed to reexamine its 1966 transportation plan and to design a new plan that would meet the present and future needs of the area's residents.

The task facing the Joint Technical Committee was a mammoth one. Existing transportation policies had to be thoroughly reviewed and recommendations concerning new and improved transportation facilities had to be made. It was also necessary to ensure that the public was informed of the issues involved and that public opinion concerning transportation policies was taken into consideration. The long-drawn-out Spadina debate had done more than anything to demonstrate the fact that the public wanted to be involved in such matters. Recognition of this fact was contained in one of the terms of reference approved by Metro Council for the Joint Technical Committee. Special emphasis, the council stated, must be placed on the need "to publicly air the issues surrounding transportation decisions so that the public may be more fully informed on matters of utmost importance to the vitality of their municipality."

In order to accomplish the Joint Technical Committee's objectives, the provincial government and Metro Toronto agreed to set up the Metropolitan Toronto Transportation Plan Review with a staff of highly qualified transportation experts. The work of this group took three years to complete. Throughout this time numerous transportation studies were undertaken and many public meetings were held. Because of the high degree of interest in the review, these public meetings were well attended. Members of the public were anxious to learn what the experts were thinking about the issues under consideration and to let the review staff know their own feelings on these issues. A great variety of opinion was evident at most of the public meetings. People opposed to expressways argued that if improved public transit facilities were provided throughout the Metro area, there would be little or no need for expressways. At the other extreme, the review staff heard arguments favoring the completion of the Spadina Expressway, the extension of existing expressways, and the building of new expressways. In addition to the people arguing for more public transit or more expressways, there was also a strong body of opinion recommending the adoption by Metro of a balanced transportation system. Such a system was seen as including both improved public transit and road facilities, including expressways, thus allowing Metro residents to choose the form of transportation most convenient to their needs.

The studies undertaken by the Metropolitan Toronto Transportation Plan Review were aimed at establishing the transportation needs of the Metro area residents, and the relative social and economic costs of providing the various facilities to meet these needs. The economic costs–the amount of money necessary to build and maintain an expressway or a subway–were considerably easier to establish than were the social costs. An example of a social cost was the number of homes, commercial buildings, or parkland that would have to be destroyed to make way for an expressway or a subway. The amount of pollution resulting from the provision of alternative transportation facilities had also to be measured and considered as a social cost. Not only was it extremely difficult to know all of the possible social costs involved, but it was equally difficult to decide upon an actual cost or dollar figure for those that were identified. For example, although an amount of money could be assigned for replacing a home, it was virtually impossible to assign a cost for the mental anguish suffered by people coerced into vacating their homes because of expressway or subway construction.

In the making of any transportation recommendation, the review staff had to consider also "The Conflict between the City and the Suburbs" issue. In its final report released in 1975, *Choices for the Future: Summary Report*, the Metropolitan Toronto Transportation Plan

Review devoted one section to the reasons for and the implications of this conflict. It arose, the report stated, because of the differing transportation objectives held by city residents and suburban residents. The Spadina debate was a particular example of these differences, with the suburbs wanting the expressway to provide fast, efficient transportation into the downtown area, and the city residents opposing the expressway because they wanted to preserve their neighborhoods and limit the number of cars entering the downtown area. "The City," the report noted, "generally wishes to discourage through traffic destined for the Central Area whereas the suburban communities . . . are dependent upon the Central Area for their employment opportunities." Designing a transportation plan to satisfy the needs and objectives of both city and suburban residents was not possible in the review staff's estimation. Therefore, in making their recommendations they were aware that "many proposals for the improvement of transportation service or the introduction of new facilities are likely to be viewed differently by City of Toronto and Metropolitan Toronto organizations and elected officials."

The Spadina Extension Is Recommended and Approved: 1975

The assumption that the report's recommendations would not be greeted with unanimous agreement by all Metro residents certainly proved to be true. Receiving the most attention was the recommendation that served to illustrate the city/suburb conflict, stating that ". . . serious consideration be given to extending the [Spadina] Expressway as a four-lane arterial road between Lawrence and Eglinton avenues, with single-lane ramps providing access both eastbound and westbound along Eglinton Avenue." Although this recommendation was only one of many aimed at improving transportation facilities within Metro, it was the one that rated headlines in local newspapers as soon as the report was released. Once again the pro- and anti-Spadina forces were mobilized to support and oppose the recommendation.

There was one noticeable difference in this renewed fight over the Spadina Expressway. In the previous phases of the battle, the main source of opposition had come from organized groups and committees of ordinary citizens; in this new phase, it came from City of Toronto Council. While it was true that certain city aldermen had steadfastly opposed the expressway throughout the years leading up to Premier Davis's 1971 decision, these aldermen had represented a minority viewpoint. By January 1975, however, they were in a majority position on city council because in the municipal elections of 1972 and 1974, aldermen supporting the expressway had either not run for office or had been defeated by candidates supporting the aims and objectives of the anti-Spadina groups. And once the Metropolitan Toronto Transportation Plan Review's final report was released, these aldermen made it clear that they would oppose any attempts to extend the expressway southwards. Naturally, their stand was fully supported by the anti-Spadina organizations.

Metro Council was the first scene in the renewed debate over the Spadina Expressway. Within weeks of receiving the Metropolitan Toronto Transportation Plan Review's final report, the recommendation concerning the paving of the expressway from Lawrence to Eglinton was being discussed by the council's boroughs and city representatives. While the city's representatives on the council opposed the recommendation, a majority of Metro councillors supported it. Throughout the debate, the city's representatives voiced their concern that if this section was paved, it would re-open the whole Spadina question and bring renewed efforts to complete the expressway into the downtown area. They pointed out that as Metro still owned the Spadina right of way (the land on which the expressway was planned to run southwards from Eglinton Avenue), further extension of the Spadina would always be a distinct possibility. Those councillors favoring the paving of the "Davis ditch" argued that such concern was unnecessary. Paving the ditch was, they said, the only sensible thing to do and the fear that the expressway would be extended even further south was groundless. Also, the paved section between Lawrence and Eglinton could not be classified as an expressway. Rather it would be a four-lane arterial road, in keeping with the Metropolitan Toronto Transportation Plan Review's recommendation. The allowable speed for cars travelling on this section would be considerably less than that allowed on expressways but would be the same as for other arterial roads. None of these assurances, however, were sufficient to satisfy the city aldermen or to diminish their fears. But they were outnumbered on Metro Council—and when a vote for approval of the paving recommendation was taken it passed easily. Metro then lost no time in notifying paving contractors that tenders for the job should be submitted as soon as possible.

The Ditch Is Paved: 1976

Residents of the streets surrounding Lawrence Avenue were delighted that at long last the "ditch" was to be paved, and that their local streets would no longer be clogged by cars entering and leaving the expressway ramps at Lawrence. But removing the problem from their area would shift the same problem one-and-a-quarter miles southwards to the local streets around Eglinton Avenue. As residents from these streets realized that all traffic entering and exiting from the Spadina would have to drive through their streets, they too formed groups to oppose the paving. Even people who had supported the expressway as it was originally planned

Levels of Government, Appointed Officials, Professional Experts and Citizens' Groups Involved in the Spadina Expressway Issue

*Replaced in 1975 by the Metro Planning Committee.

found themselves opposed to it when it was going to end, so to speak, in their backyards.

Toronto City Council, with the support of various citizen groups, decided in May 1975 to make a personal appeal to Premier Davis and request him to halt the paving. They were confident that the premier would grant their request because of his earlier Spadina decision. Instead, Premier Davis made it quite clear that he approved of the plan to extend the Spadina to Eglinton. His approval was not, in his opinion, a reversal of his stop-Spadina decision because the new section would be an arterial road and not an expressway. "I think there is a difference between an expressway like the Macdonald Cartier Freeway and a four-lane road," he said, justifying his position. However, to help overcome the fears that the Spadina would, at some later date, be extended even further southwards, Premier Davis announced a set of protective guarantees, aimed at preventing such an eventuality. The guarantees promised included a commitment by the province to remove the Spadina right of way from Metro's authority and to provide for the City of Toronto a three-foot-wide [about 1 m] strip of land across the right of way—provisions that would make any further extension to the expressway impossible. To prevent traffic problems on the local streets surrounding Eglinton, Premier Davis also promised that his government would share with Metro the cost of building a parking facility at either the Eglinton or Lawrence subway station "or at some intermediate points between." This parking facility would be designed to encourage motorists to park their cars and use the subway for travelling into the downtown area. In addition, the premier requested Metro to provide a traffic plan for the area south of Eglinton "to ensure that traffic generated by the Spadina arterial road will remain on other Metro arterial roads rather than on local roads."

None of these protective measures were sufficient to

persuade city council members and other Spadina opponents to give up their fight. Concern was expressed that because the premier had, in their opinion, gone back on his earlier decision on Spadina, he was also likely not to fulfill the various promises he had made to prevent further extension of Spadina. Despair over the provincial government's seriousness forced the City of Toronto to examine other avenues of appeal. Only one was open and that was to lodge an appeal against paving the ditch with the Supreme Court of Ontario. This appeal was rejected in April 1975. The city's solicitor then advised the council members that further legal action would be fruitless. In desperation, a delegation from the city requested a meeting with Premier Davis. At the meeting, held on 17 May 1976, the premier again refused to stop the paving, and in a statement released to the press he repeated his government's promises to act in such a way as to prevent the Spadina being extended south of Eglinton.

Early the following morning the paving contractors arrived at the ditch side ready to commence work. They were greeted by anti-Spadina supporters who planned to prevent the workers from doing their job. But their efforts to stop the paving were in vain. Those who did not leave voluntarily were dragged away by policemen brought in to clear the site. Once this was done the paving of the Spadina ditch began. It was not a long job and by July 1976 the Spadina arterial road was in use by motorists. Anti-Spadina supporters could only hope that the provincial government would make good on its promises to prevent any further extension.

Demands for an extension continued, not only by people who had always supported the building of the expressway but also by people who now lived in streets located around the end of the Spadina arterial road. Despite the implementation of a traffic plan for these streets, residents complained about the considerably increased traffic in their neighborhood. And motorists using the expressway expressed anger and frustration at the frequent traffic jams caused by cars trying to enter and exit from the new arterial road. For many, the only solution was to complete the expressway as planned into the downtown area, thus providing a number of exit and entrance ramps for traffic using the expressway to travel into and out of the city. Anti-Spadina supporters, concerned by the growing support for extending the road, argued that the building of a parking facility where motorists could leave their cars and use the subway (which opened in 1977) would alleviate the problems resulting from the abrupt ending of the Spadina. But the borough and city politicians involved in discussions about the building of a parking facility could not come to any agreement about its location. City politicians felt that the boroughs were more interested in extending Spadina than in providing parking space for motorists where the road stopped. By 1980 the situation was still unresolved; Spadina stopped at Eglinton and no plans for a parking facility had been agreed upon.

Officially the debate over Spadina finished once the road was paved down to Eglinton. Unofficially, the debate would never end. It had raised so many controversial issues that in the future, wherever and whenever urban transportation was being discussed by people from Metro and from other large cities, they would always refer to the Spadina Expressway. The Spadina had been a centre of attention when it was first built by William Warren Baldwin. Over one hundred and seventy years later, for different reasons, it was to remain so.

The Issues VI

- Should the expressway be completed as planned into downtown Toronto?

Social Costs

• Throughout the Spadina debate opponents of the expressway argued that, if it was completed as planned, downtown Toronto would eventually become another Los Angeles where, according to Jane Jacobs, the noted urbanologist, ". . . exhausts have turned the air into a crisis, where expressways, interchanges and parking lots occupy some two thirds of the drained and vacuous downtown."

- -Is the comparison of Toronto with Los Angeles a fair one?
- -Is it inevitable that car pollution and a large number of parking lots will be found in the centre of large cities? Why? Why not?
- -Are there not ways of controlling traffic in downtown areas through the imposition of high parking rates and the provision of good public transport?

• Were the residents of downtown neighborhoods justified in opposing plans for the Spadina Expressway because

- -it would pass through their communities?
- -destroy some homes in their communities?
- -they believed it would increase air and noise pollution in their communities?

• Which position is stronger and why?

- -that of the Spadina opponents who claimed that cars entering and exiting from the expressway would destroy their neighborhood by increasing traffic and pollution on local, residential streets

  or

- -that of the Spadina supporters who claimed that the expressway would reduce existing traffic and pollution on local streets by providing an alternative, faster route for motorists.

• Does not living in a downtown area have its benefits, such as being close to shops, entertainment, jobs, and so on, and its drawbacks such as increased traffic? Do not these benefits and drawbacks go together?

- Was it selfish of downtown residents who lived within easy access of public transit facilities to oppose an expressway that would be used by suburban residents who lacked easy access to such facilities?
- Is it more important to preserve neighborhoods than to provide fast roads for motorists who need them?

Parallel Situation: Destruction of the Amish Lifestyle by Modern Technology

The Old Order Amish are an ultraconservative sect of the Mennonite religious order. A number of Amish communities have lived and worked as dairy farmers in southwestern Ontario for many years. Some of these communities were established by Amish families who left the U.S. during the American Revolution and Civil War when government attempts to conscript them into the army threatened to undermine their pacifist beliefs. Throughout the latter part of the nineteenth and early twentieth centuries the original settlers were joined by groups of Amish from various European countries seeking refuge from similar threats to their pacifist beliefs.

The Amish adapted well to their new country. Until 1976 their existence was a peaceful one, revolving around their work and religion. In June of that year, however, this existence was once again threatened when the Ontario government announced the introduction of new dairy farming regulations. These new regulations, that were to come into effect on 1 November 1977, required all of the province's dairy farmers to store and ship their milk in electrically cooled bulk containers rather than in the traditional steel milk cans still used by many farmers, including the Amish. According to the government these new methods were intended to make milk production more hygienic and efficient, thus reducing the cost to consumers. But to the Amish, whose faith forbids the use of electricity, these new regulations were viewed as government interference with their whole way of life.

The Amish objected not only to the use of electricity but also to the use of any form of mechanization. In 1976 they were still working their fields behind hand-drawn ploughs and harvesters, and milking their cows by hand. Farming was seen as a family activity with all members expected to do their share of the chores. "The ban against mechanization," explained an Amish spokesman, "keeps everyone occupied so that sons and daughters do not go off to the city looking for jobs." The Amish feared that if they allowed the use of electricity on their farms, eventually they would be forced to introduce other types of mechanized farming devices. This, they argued, would mean fewer jobs for their sons and daughters who would then leave the farms to seek city jobs where outside influences would corrupt their religious beliefs and practices.

In order to preserve their traditional lifestyle the Amish decided to ask the Ontario Milk Marketing Board, the provincial agency responsible for implementing the new regulations, to grant them a special exemption status. The milk board refused the request, claiming that the traditional stainless steel cans used by the Amish were unsafe and could no longer meet Ontario health standards. The Amish promised to match any hygiene standards set up by the board and, if these standards were unsatisfactory, they were prepared to have the board reject their milk. The board refused this offer, arguing that if the Amish were granted an exemption from the new regulations then other farmers, who were reluctant to accept the new methods, would demand similar consideration.

At the same time, board members denied accusations that they were trying to put the Amish farmers out of business and pointed out that a number of alternatives had been suggested. Among these were that the Amish turn either to cream production, where steel cans were still acceptable, or to raising swine. The Amish were unhappy with both suggestions. Cream products relied heavily on government subsidies and the Amish would not accept subsidies, just as they would not accept pension cheques or welfare. The idea that they should raise and slaughter hogs was at even greater odds with their way of life.

The plight of the Amish brought much support from the general public. Eventually the Milk Marketing Board agreed to a compromise solution, whereby the Amish farmers would be allowed to install communal bulk refrigerated coolers, powered by diesel generators, to hold and chill their milk. However, only existing farmers were to be permitted to use this method. This ruling meant, therefore, that it would be impossible for young Amish farmers to take over their family businesses or to start one of their own. To the Amish, who had preserved their communities intact and largely unchanged throughout the twentieth century, the board's compromise offer did little to solve their problems. Rather than face the prospect of having their sons and daughters unable to continue their traditional lifestyles, many Amish families decided to sell their farms and to head for an established Amish community in Pennsylvania. There, they said, the government would not interfere.

- Have the rights of the Amish been violated in the same way as the rights of residents in an established community through which an expressway is planned to run?

- Is the potential threat posed by the new dairy farming regulations to the Amish's traditional lifestyle sufficient reason to exempt them from these regulations?

- Since the Amish have lived in their own way for a long time, running their farms without the use of electricity or any form of mechanization and holding onto their traditional religious customs, do you believe they should have the right to continue their way of life undisturbed?

- As the Amish own their farms, do not they alone have the right to decide how they will run them?

- If farm conditions are intolerable and inhumane, and food production methods are unsanitary, does not the government have a responsibility to discontinue the operation? If certain foods (e.g., milk and eggs), are being overproduced and would be wasted, should their production be regulated and restricted by the government?

- If the Amish could meet the government's new health standards without resorting to the use of electricity should they be exempted from the new regulations? Should other farmers be similarly exempted provided that they too can meet the new health standards? Would it not make the administration of the law too cumbersome if too many exemptions were made?

- Should the Milk Marketing Board's compromise offer be restricted only to existing Amish farmers or should any future farmer, who so desires, be allowed to use this method for cooling and storing milk?

- Do the traditional farming methods used by the Amish represent an undesirable form of production in modern-day society?

  Is it unrealistic for the Amish to want to hold onto their traditional farming methods? Is it wrong? Why? Why not?

- Do the Amish objections to the new regulations represent an attempt to stop inevitable progress? Do they have a right to stop progress in the light of their religious beliefs?

- Do you think that a majority, as represented by an elected government, has the right to make decisions that will change the lifestyle of a minority?

- In what way(s) is the plight of the Amish dairy farmers in southwestern Ontario similar to that of the residents of downtown neighborhoods through which the Spadina Expressway was planned to run? In what way(s) is it different?

- According to what principle would you decide when governments should be allowed to make decisions that affect people's lifestyles and when the right of people to maintain their own lifestyle should be respected?

Personal Preferences

- Does the fact that moving out to live in the suburbs was a personal choice made by residents of Toronto's northwest suburbs justify the designing and completion of the Spadina Expressway to serve their needs?

- If adequate public transit facilities are available for travelling to work, shop, entertainment, and so on, and people still prefer to drive their own cars, do local authorities have an obligation to provide good roads for car users?

- Do people living in large urban areas have the right to drive their cars whenever and wherever they wish? Is this a right or a privilege? Are there any limits on this right? Should governments have the right to restrict car use if pollution reaches unacceptable levels?

- Given society's needs to conserve energy should governments enact legislation aimed at restricting car ownership and use? If so, what kind of restriction would you recommend?

Parallel Situation

In recent years some Canadian cities have banned cars from parts of their downtown areas to create pedestrian malls. But while successful malls can now be enjoyed in such cities as Calgary and Ottawa, Toronto has failed in its attempts to set up a car-free area along downtown Yonge Street. During the summer of 1971, Toronto City Council began its first experiment with a pedestrian mall that lasted for four weeks. Similar experiments occurred throughout the following three summers. For some people the absence of cars proved to be delightful; for others, it proved to be an inconvenience that was totally intolerable. Many car owners complained that the local council had no right to impose restrictions on where they could use their cars. These complaints were also backed up by a number of downtown merchants who argued that their businesses dropped off considerably when people were unable to drive to and from their stores. As a result of this opposition the Toronto City Council decided against turning part of Yonge Street into a permanent pedestrian mall.

- Do you agree with the decision not to have a permanent pedestrian mall on downtown Yonge Street? Why? Why not?
- Does the Toronto City Council have a responsibility to compensate storeowners for the losses they claim to have suffered while the pedestrian malls were in operation?
- If adequate public transportation facilities are available for people to travel to downtown areas should they still expect to be able to drive there?
- Should downtown merchants contribute to the cost of providing such transportation facilities?

Research Activity

Spadina Expressway opponents claimed that most people would prefer to use good public transit facilities rather than drive their own cars. Survey the students in your classroom to establish whether or not they agree with this claim.

Man, Machines, and Democracy

• In his minority report on the 1971 OMB Spadina decision, Mr. J. A. Kennedy remarked that "machines are made to serve man, not man machines, regardless of whether the machine is an automobile or a computer. Surely democracy (freedom of choice in how to travel) does not dictate that an expressway must be cut through quiet development in a city. . . ."

- -Do you agree with the implications of these remarks that those favoring the completion of the Spadina Expressway will become servants of the automobile? or
- -Could one argue, reasonably, that the building of any expressway, including the Spadina, shows how machines become the servant of man insofar as a technology is used to minister to modern-day life-styles?

• Premier Davis justified his cabinet's decision to stop the Spadina Expressway by stating that "if we are building a transportation system to serve the automobile, the Spadina Expressway is a good place to start. But if we are building a transportation system to serve people, the Spadina Expressway is a good place to stop."

- -Is Premier Davis correct in assuming that the expressway would serve the automobile and not human needs?
- -Does stopping its construction serve people more than machines?
- -Would you agree with the view that both the starting and the stopping of the Spadina Expressway serve some human needs and restrict others?
- -Which human needs can best be served by the building of such an expressway and which are best served by stopping it? On balance, which of these needs do you consider to be most important and why?

The Stop Spadina Decision

- Was the decision to stop the expressway at Lawrence Avenue justified when
  - -the section between Lawrence and Eglinton had already been cleared and prepared for paving?
  - -over 60 million dollars had already been spent on construction?
- Should this unpaved section of the expressway have been
  - -completed as originally planned?
  - -completed as a four-lane arterial road?
  - -left incomplete and used for some purpose other than a road or an expressway?

  Give reasons to support your answers.
- Should people living near the entrance and exit ramps of expressways receive financial compensation for the inconveniences they suffer? If so, who should provide such compensation?
- By paving the Spadina to Eglinton Avenue, were the problems caused by increased traffic on local streets solved? Should cars entering and exiting from major expressways be banned from residential streets? How would you suggest such a ban be implemented?

Parallel Situation

Moore Park is a middle-class residential area located in midtown Toronto. Its proximity to good schools, shops, and public transportation make it an attractive place to live for those who can afford to buy a home there. For many residents the only disadvantage in their location was heavy use of local streets by commuters driving through the area en route to and from work. As a result of complaints from the Moore Park Ratepayers' Association, the Toronto City Council approved a traffic plan for the area that involved closing most of the local streets to through traffic during morning and evening rush hours. Cars needing to travel through this part of the city during these times must now use only certain main streets to do so. But while these traffic regulations have made the residents of the restricted access streets happy, they have greatly annoyed people living on the area's few main streets who have to put up with increased traffic, noise, and car-pollution fumes. And commuters, forced to use these main streets, complain about the inconvenience, the daily traffic jams, and the resulting longer journeys to and from work.

- Do any of the residents of Moore Park have a right to expect that their streets will be free of traffic at certain times of the day?

- Should the residents of some streets in the area enjoy the peace and quiet of traffic-free streets while residents on nearby streets have to live with considerably increased amounts of traffic?

- Is it right to restrict access to streets for commuters or anyone else? Are such restrictions compatible with the right of people to go where they want to? Are they more important?

- Given that all the streets in Moore Park are public property, does not the local authority have an obligation to ensure that they are open to the use of all citizens engaged in a legal activity (e.g., driving a car)?

- If the use of a public street is restricted to a few people for all or part of a day is it not fair to say that the people living there are receiving a grant of public property at the expense of all other people who need it?

- Can you suggest any alternative solutions to the traffic problem in Moore Park? What are they and what advantages do they have over the current regulations?

Alternatives

- Do you think that Metro Toronto should widen existing roads rather than build the Spadina or any other expressway? Why? Why not?

- Would you still agree to the widening of existing roads even if this
  - -cost more than building expressways?
  - -involved cutting down trees?
  - -meant destroying houses?
  - -meant reducing or eliminating sidewalks?

- If you lived in northwestern Metro and worked in downtown Toronto would you
  - -drive your car to a subway parking lot and then continue your journey by subway?
  - -expect public transit facilities, either bus or subway, to be provided from your home to your place of work?
  - -use the existing roads to drive to work?
  - -continue to press for the completion of the Spadina expressway?

Summary Questions

- According to Mr. Robert McGuire, a member of the OMB panel that approved the decision to complete the Spadina Expressway, "The right of citizens to advise cannot be interpreted as the right to supplant the decision making body Metro Council as the recognized political formation in our society, or otherwise chaos would result. . . ."
  - -Could the form that the citizen opposition took to the Spadina Expressway be interpreted as supplanting the authority of Metro Council? How?
  - -Should not citizens be allowed to oppose and campaign against issues being considered by local or any other government authorities?

- Who do you think should have made the final decision to complete or to stop the Spadina Expressway
  - -Metro Council?

-Toronto City Council?
-The OMB?
-The provincial government?
-The Metro planners?
-All of the residents of Metro through a public referendum?
-Some other group or individuals?
Support your answers with reasons.

• If it could be proved to your satisfaction that expressways in urban areas do reduce traffic and car and noise pollution on ordinary roads would you recommend that a network of expressways be built that provides access to all areas of the city and to one another?

• Given that in most Canadian cities there is a shortage of vacant land and a limited amount of public money available for the building of roads and public transit facilities, how do you strike a balance between the need for roads and public transit facilities and peoples' overwhelming desire to drive their own cars?

THE SPADINA EXPRESSWAY

Summary of Key Developments		Key Decisions	
Post World War II 1945	Development of new subdivisions northwest of Toronto creates demand for a northwest expressway linking the subdivisions with downtown Toronto.		
1953	The Ontario provincial government creates the municipality of Metropolitan Toronto, an amalgamation of the city of Toronto and its surrounding boroughs and townships.		
1953–61	Metro's Planning Board and Department of Roads develop plans and recommendations for improving Metro's road system that include plans for the Spadina Expressway.		
		Dec. 1961	Metro Council approves Metro Planning Board's recommendation to construct the first one-and-a-half mile section of the Expressway from Highway 401 to Lawrence Avenue.

Summary of Key Developments		Key Decisions	
Dec. 1961 to Feb. 1962	Heated public debate in newspapers over plans to construct Spadina leads to revelation of Yorkdale connection.		
		Summer 1963	The Ontario Municipal Board (OMB) approves plans for constructing the first section of the Expressway.
1966 The first section of the Spadina Expressway is opened			
1966–69	Plans are drawn up to extend the Expressway south and the section from Lawrence to Eglinton is readied for paving. Citizen opposition to Spadina grows and the Stop Spadina Save Our City Committee (SSSOCC) is formed in October 1969.		
		Sept. 1969	Metro Council halts Spadina construction and requests Metro Planning Board to report on the Expressway.

March 1970	Metro Planning Board Report on Expressway recommends its completion into downtown Toronto.
April/May 1970	Public hearings on Report are held.
May 1970	Metro Transportation Committee refuses City of Toronto request for an independent inquiry on the future of Spadina.
Aug. 1970	Anti-Expressway supporters retain lawyer and request OMB to review its 1963 Spadina decision.
Jan. 1971	The OMB holds an independent inquiry into the Spadina project; pro- and anti-Expressway supporters present their cases.
June 1970	Metro Council approves Metro Planning Board's recommendation for completing Expressway.
Aug. 1970	Metro Council requests OMB approval for completing Expressway.
Feb. 1971	The OMB votes two to one in favor of completing the Expressway.

Summary of Key Developments		Key Decisions	
Feb. 1971	Anti-Spadina supporters appeal OMB decision to the provincial cabinet.		
		June 1971	The provincial cabinet overturns OMB decision and stops the Expressway at Lawrence Avenue.
July 1971 to March 1975	Pro-Spadina groups urge paving of Expressway from Lawrence to Eglinton.		
Feb. 1972	Metro Toronto Transportation Review set up to study Metro's transportation needs.		
Jan. 1975	Metro Toronto Transportation Review recommends paving the Expressway from Lawrence to Eglinton as a four-lane arterial road.		
		March 1975	Metro Council approves recommendation for paving Spadina from Lawrence to Eglinton.
May 1975 to May 1976	Anti-Spadina supporters unsuccessfully oppose Metro's decision to pave Expressway.		

July 1976 the Spadina arterial road from Lawrence to Eglinton is opened

1976 to present	Pro-Spadina supporters continue to urge completion of Spadina into downtown Toronto.

2 URBAN POLLUTION

Canada Metal Company

For years Bon Weii Lee and his wife lived in an apartment and dreamed of owning their own house complete with a backyard. After years of saving they finally realized their dream in the spring of 1973 when they and their children moved into a small house in an old established section in Toronto's east end. None of the houses in this area were palatial but nearly all of them had yards that were carefully tended by their owners. Shortly after they moved in the Lees were busy planting lots of Chinese green vegetables in their yard. Not only did this give them much pleasure, but they also hoped that growing their own vegetables would be a lot cheaper than buying them. With all their money invested in their house, Mr. and Mrs. Lee needed to economize wherever possible.

By midsummer the Lees noticed brown burn marks appearing on the leaves of their vegetables. Mr. Lee asked his neighbors if they knew what the cause might be. The neighbors did not know and pointed to similar marks on their own plants and vegetables. Such marks were common, the Lees' neighbors assured them, and really did not mean that there was anything wrong. So, although the Chinese greens did not look as attractive as the store-bought variety, the Lees harvested them and ate them.

A few weeks later a report released by the Ontario Ministry of the Environment gave the Lees and their neighbors the first official indication about why their plants and vegetables were scarred with brown marks. The report showed that in tests taken during the previous summer, government officials had found the lead content of dustfall was 49 tons per square mile in the area where the Lees lived; a reading of 13 tons was considered normal. Samples of soil taken from yards in the area had shown high levels of lead contamination; similarly high levels of lead pollutant had also been found in the air. Although the government report was hesitant to cite a cause for its findings, it did suggest that a relationship might exist between the high lead levels in the soil and air and the presence in the area of a lead-smelting factory, the Canada Metal Company.

Once the government's findings were made public, the newspapers, radio, and television stations reported at length on the possible dangers of lead pollution to human beings. People living in lead-polluted areas, the Lees and their neighbors discovered, could contract lead poisoning by inhaling lead from the air or by eating produce grown in lead-contaminated soil. Such produce, the Lees learned to their horror, normally had brown marks on the leaves. Lead poisoning, the various reports pointed out, was a very dangerous and, in some cases, fatal disease. In mild cases it caused colic, stomach pains, anemia, and bloody diarrhea; in severe cases it caused brain damage and the destruction of life-supporting red blood cells.

The release of the lead-pollution report and the accounts of the effects of lead poisoning brought demands for immediate testing of the area's residents to determine if any of them had contracted the disease. A voluntary program for testing residents' blood was organized by the City of Toronto's Board of Health. To ensure that all of the children who lived in the area were tested, the Toronto Board of Education also arranged for public health officials to take blood samples at the local public school. As a result of these tests doctors found 23 children with blood lead levels excessively higher than the 20 to 30 micrograms of lead per cubic centimeter of blood considered normal for city residents. In one family, twelve-year-old twins John and Ted Regina had lead levels in their blood of 50 micrograms, while their eight-year-old brother Robert had 135 micrograms. The 23 children were admitted to hospital for observation. Of these, 18 were sent home within a few days while the remaining five were kept in for treatment for mild forms of lead poisoning. The parents of these children were advised by medical officials to move away from the area to prevent their children from further exposure to lead pollution.

Both Mr. and Mrs. Lee were tested along with their children and were extremely relieved when the results were negative. But the Lees realized that if they continued to live in the area and nothing was done about the pollution, it was highly likely that in a few years' time the results would not be negative. They thought about moving but simply could not afford to do so. In this respect they were no different from the vast majority of the people living in the area, few of whom had the money to move away. Those families who were specifically advised to find houses elsewhere tried to do so, but gave up because of the expense. Frustration over their seeming inability to do anything about the situation gradually gave way to a demand by the area's residents that the provincial government close down the Canada Metal Company. The Toronto Board of Health backed the residents' demand.

The release of two new studies documenting the incidence of lead pollution in the area helped to strengthen this demand. The studies, one by the Ministry of the Environment and one by the University of Toronto's Institute of Environmental Studies, were almost identical in their findings and fully confirmed the results of the earlier study. In fact the lead content of the area's dustfall had increased to 70 tons per square mile since the original testing was done. Furthermore, both of these new studies reported that comparative studies undertaken in other areas of the city, where there were no lead smelting plants, showed lead content dustfall readings ranging from only .01 to .07 tons per square mile. With this evidence in hand, the provincial government exercised its power (granted by the 1971 Environmental Protection Act) to close down factories found to be excessively polluting the environment and ordered the immediate shutdown of the Canada Metal Company.

Angry protests from company officials, union representatives, and workers greeted the government's order. Company officials denied that their factory was a major source of pollution, and accused the government of ignoring the fact that a large amount of the lead pollution in the air resulted not from their factory's activities but rather from the emission of fumes from cars using leaded gasoline. Furthermore, they claimed that their company had a long history of pollution control and was willing to work with the Ministry of the Environment to reduce pollution levels still further. Union officials and workers at the plant, angered by the sudden closure and subsequent loss of their wages, picketed the offices of the Toronto Board of Health and the Ontario Ministry of the Environment demanding that the factory be reopened. Within a few weeks the provincial government announced that the Canada Metal Company had agreed to install a new filtering system, designed to reduce lead emissions into the air, and would therefore be allowed to reopen.

After the new filtering system was installed, further government studies of lead pollution in the atmosphere were carried out. These showed that although the additional pollution controls had succeeded in reducing the level of lead in the area, the amounts that were present in both the air and the soils remained excessively high and were still dangerous to human beings. At the same time, government studies of two other city areas in which lead-smelting factories were located reported that both areas had unacceptably high lead levels in the atmosphere. Comparative studies were also undertaken of areas that did not have lead-smelting plants in their midst but were similar in terms of ethnic composition, the amount of traffic using the streets, and the number of people living there. None of these areas exhibited high levels of lead pollution, which gave further strength to the argument that lead-smelting plants were a major source of such pollution.

The increasing evidence that companies such as Canada Metal were putting excessively dangerous amounts of lead into the atmosphere resulted in a fresh outbreak of newspaper stories detailing the horrors of lead poisoning, and CBC radio announced that it had prepared a special program on the subject. The program, entitled "Dying of Lead," promised to release alarming facts on the incidence of lead pollution and its effects. Before it was broadcast, however, the Canada Metal Company, together with one of the other lead smelting companies, successfully brought an injunction against the CBC to stop the program from going on the air. Company officials claimed that the CBC's program was biassed and libelous insofar as it made no attempt to present an objective assessment of the situation.

The companies' success in forcing the CBC to cancel the program caused an angry reaction from public officials and private citizens. Dr. David Parkinson, a doctor at Sick Children's Hospital and a member of the

Toronto Board of Health, echoed the feelings of many people when he suggested that the efforts of ordinary people to do something about lead pollution were hopeless in the face of the "high-powered lawyers and public relations firms" hired by the lead-smelting companies. The Toronto Board of Health decided to ask the provincial government for financial assistance to help move families away from the polluted area. The provincial government was also requested to replace the lead contaminated soils in the affected areas. Rather than agree to these requests, the government announced that it would hold a public hearing on lead pollution before deciding what action, if any, was necessary.

The public hearing opened in January 1975 and lasted for over six months. During this time many briefs were presented and many expert witnesses were called to testify. Among the latter was Dr. Henrietta Sachs, a U.S. pediatrician and medical expert in the diagnosis and treatment of lead poisoning. She appeared as a witness for the lead-smelting companies, and in her testimony she claimed that the only serious cause of lead poisoning in children came through eating leaded paint. Children can, she said, "tolerate what they get in the air very, very well." The extent to which children could tolerate lead pollution in the air was disputed in a brief presented by the Toronto Board of Education. This brief pointed out that, while only a few children living near the lead-smelting plants had required hospital treatment for lead poisoning, approximately 400 children had been found to have blood lead levels higher than those found in children living in other areas of the city. And there was, the Board of Education suggested, a strong possibility that many of these 400 children were suffering from some side effects of lead poisoning that were not easily diagnosed by medical experts. Lead poisoning, the brief continued, did not always result in such obvious physical symptoms as colic, bloody diarrhea, and so on, but was also known to cause psychological and neurological impairment leading to hyperactivity in children as well as reading and writing difficulties. The Board of Education's brief maintained that these lesser known side effects of lead pollution were difficult to detect but were, nevertheless, serious and should not be ignored. In conclusion, the brief urged the province to require more stringent controls for lead-polluting industries and to initiate a cleanup of the lead-contaminated soils in the affected areas.

A brief presented by the City of Toronto backed up the Board of Education's request for tighter pollution controls. This brief also noted that under present zoning laws lead-smelting factories would not be allowed to operate in residential areas. However, because plants such as the Canada Metal Company had been in existence before the present zoning laws had been approved, the city had no legal power to close them down or order them to move. Despite the legality of their operations, the city suggested that all lead-smelting companies located in residential areas had a responsibility to ensure that their activities did not endanger the health of people living nearby.

The report of the public hearing into lead pollution was released in December 1975. In it the provincial officials stated that they could find no evidence of a direct relationship between lead poisoning and lead pollution caused by the lead-smelting factories. The cases of lead poisoning that had been discovered, the report maintained, could have been caused by other sources such as eating leaded paint. It was, the report admitted, extremely difficult to isolate the cause of high lead levels in a person's blood. Nevertheless, the report recommended that the lead smelting companies should be made to pay for the removal of lead-contaminated soil in the affected areas and its replacement with clean soil. Parents were also advised to warn their children not to eat the soil or any vegetation grown in it. Continued testing of the blood lead levels of young children and pregnant mothers was also advised. Such testing, the report noted, should also be carried out on all workers in lead plants. At the same time the Ministry of the Environment was urged to continue monitoring the affected areas to check the amounts of lead pollution present, and some specific recommendations with regard to the enclosure, unloading, and handling of lead-bearing materials were made. The report concluded by stating that its recommendations, if adopted, would minimize any threat to public health caused by the presence of the lead-smelting companies, and that there was, therefore, no justification for closing them down or for providing financial assistance to help families relocate to other parts of the city.

Despite this reassurance, many people remained unconvinced that living near a lead-smelting plant posed no threat to their health. But lacking the necessary financial resources to move, they could only stay put and hope that the report's recommendations would be implemented. Government attempts to have the companies clean up the lead-contaminated soils failed and many homeowners went ahead and did this on their own. In 1977, the provincial government decided to use $70 000 of provincial lottery money to pay for the cleanup. Homeowners were reimbursed for their expense and the lead-smelting companies, after lengthy negotiations with the provincial government, agreed to pay one-third of the cost of the cleanup operation.

Within a year of the cleanup operation, it became clear that lead pollution remained a problem for people living near the Canada Metal Company. Readings taken by Ministry of the Environment officials showed that on fifteen successive days during October 1978 the lead levels in the air near the plant were twice as high as those permitted by the government, and that the soil in four of the nearby homes contained excessively high amounts of lead contamination. The Ministry blamed the problem on sloppy maintenance at the plant and ordered Canada Metal officials to improve their maintenance procedures. Mr. Harry Parrot, Minister of the Environment, also promised the anxious residents of the area that the plant would be regularly inspected and that it would be closed if lead emissions were exceeded again.

These promises did little to reassure the residents, who despaired of ever living in a clean environment. Some nine months later, it was disclosed that on 15 June 1979 air pollution monitors registered lead emissions 26 times above the permissible maximum, and four times above the maximum on the following day. These disclosures lead to a tumultous meeting of angry neighborhood residents who demanded that action be taken immediately to solve the problem. The government responded by laying four minor charges of lead pollution against the company. A Canada Metal spokesman blamed the high June lead emissions on the breakdown of the plant's normal pollution control system and the failure, at the same time, of its pollution monitors. When asked why the company did not have a back-up pollution control system, the same spokesman replied that the government had never requested that one be installed. Further enquiries by newspaper reporters revealed that pollution monitor alarms had not failed on the days in question but had been dismantled for repairs.

Over the following few months residents pressed the government to admit that its previous control orders were inadequate and that new, more stringent ones must be made. In October 1979 the Minister of the Environment made a public announcement in which he stated that his Ministry's current control orders had failed because the Canada Metal Company had not maintained and operated its pollution control system properly. To remedy the situation once and for all, the Minister gave details of a new control order against the company. This new order, which was to come into effect the next month, gave Canada Metal until 15 December 1980 to complete twenty-five steps for the control of lead pollution including the installation of back-up pollution control devices. Canada Metal's president, Douglas Hutton, estimated that although the new order would cost his company $535 000 on top of the $1.5 million already spent on pollution control, his firm would co-operate with the government's directives. The government, for its part, tried to reassure the sceptical residents that this time it really intended to clean up the environment, that no exceptions would be allowed, and that if the new control system was not fully operational by the specified date the Canada Metal Company would be taken to Court.

The scepticism of the people who lived near the lead-smelting plant that their environment would ever be truly clean was shared by many others who felt that homes and pollution-potential industries should not be located near one another. This scepticism and concern were not shared by the majority of Toronto City Council, who voted in April 1980 to build an 88-unit apartment complex for low-income tenants on vacant land near the Canada Metal Company. To placate council members who opposed the project, the city agreed to have tenants in the apartments sign a lease containing a warning that "due to the presence of industrial activities in the area, odor and noise may under certain conditions annoy the occupant." Public reaction to the city's proposal was best summed up in a *Globe and Mail* editorial, which suggested that the tenants' lease also contain a warning that the ". . . soil may have to be carted away and it might be wise for them to keep their windows shut. Other than that," the editorial concluded, "it's a terrific location."

The Issues

Should the Canada Metal Company be allowed to continue its operations?

Industrial Location

• What should the government have done when it first knew about the unacceptably high levels of lead pollution in the area around the Canada Metal Company?

• Should it have closed down the factory immediately? If so, should the government have compensated the owners? Why? Why not?

• Should the Lees and the other residents in the area have been immediately relocated? If so, should they have received some form of financial compensation from the government? Why? Why not?

• Does the fact that the Canada Metal Company was legally present in the area, insofar as it conformed with the zoning regulations, give it the right to emit lead into the air because such emissions are inevitable by-products of lead-smelting operations?

• If a chemical reagent used by a chemical plant that has been in operation for 30 years is suddenly discovered to cause cancer in the plant's workers and people living nearby, would the government be justified in closing down the plant? Would the government be equally justified in closing down the plant if its operations contaminated the atmosphere with an obnoxious odor that caused discomfort to workers and nearby residents? Why? Why not?

• Since the Bon Weii Lee family decided to buy a home located near a lead-smelting plant should they expect to live in an environment that is not guaranteed to hurt their health?

- Should people be allowed to live in a heavily industrialized area even though some accommodation appropriate for housing is available there?
- Should owners of properties located in industrial areas be made legally responsible for warning prospective tenants and buyers about the potential dangers of living in such neighborhoods? Why? Why not?
- Do people living in quiet residential neighborhoods have the right to expect that their environment will not be threatened by the construction of an expressway through the area?
- Is the provision of a healthy living environment a primary obligation of all levels of government–local, provincial, and federal?

or

- Is it the responsibility of individuals to choose for themselves where they will live and accept any risks that go with it?
- Should industry that results in pollution (a) known to be, or (b) suspected of being, hazardous to health be allowed to operate in or near existing residential communities?

Employment and Pollution

Parallel Situation

In 1950, the City of Toronto had about 4000 firms employing 160 000 workers, but by 1971 the total had dwindled to 2031 firms with 82 000 workers. Most of these firms and jobs relocated in the suburbs where land was cheaper and more plentiful than in the city. As a result many people who formerly lived and worked in the city were faced with a choice of moving to the suburbs to live closer to their work or living in the city and travelling long distances to work. Many opted for neither, decided to stay put, and tried to find jobs among the rapidly dwindling opportunities available in the city. Over the years, unemployment increased dramatically, especially among the city's blue-collar workers. In an attempt to rectify the situation by halting the exodus of industry to the suburbs, Toronto City Council agreed in April 1978 to zone 1000 acres [405 hectares] of prime downtown land near the waterfront for industrial use. No restrictions were recommended for the kind of industry to be built in the area. The land thus designated for industry had previously been zoned to allow for only commercial development. Many developers who wanted to build commercial buildings–office towers, theatres, restaurants and apartment buildings–protested the city's decision. Despite these protests, city council decided to go ahead with its plans arguing that the area must be reserved exclusively for industry to provide jobs for blue-collar workers in surrounding neighborhoods.

- Do you agree that industry should be located within the City of Toronto near residential communities in order to provide jobs for city residents? Why not?

or

- Do you believe that satisfactory living environments can only be maintained if all industries are located outside of cities as far away as possible from residential communities?

- Should any kind of industry be allowed to locate in the city or should only "clean" industries that do not pollute the environment be allowed in? What effect would this have on employment? Is it better to lose jobs in order to provide a healthy living environment or to endanger the environment in order to save jobs?

- If industry is to be encouraged to locate in the city would you prefer to see it concentrated in one large area or scattered throughout the city? What kind of industries would you prefer to have (a) concentrated in one area (b) scattered throughout the city? What advantages/disadvantages are there in both types of industrial location?

• Should the city allow some limited form of commercial development on part of the 1000 acres [405 hectares] designated for industrial use? Why? Why not?

• Would you favor a decision to zone an area for industrial use if it is near good transportation facilities such as a highway and a railway and it is presently occupied by

-inexpensive housing?
-expensive housing?
-retail shops?
-office buildings?
-a park?
-movie theatres, restaurants, and so on?

Give reasons for your answers.

• Do local authorities, such as the City of Toronto, have an obligation to provide adequate employment opportunities for people who live within their boundaries? If so, should they have the legal power to decide where and how such opportunities will be provided?

Government Rights and Responsibility

• The Ontario Ministry of the Environment knew from tests taken in the summer of 1972 that unacceptably high levels of air and soil lead pollution were present in the area near the Canada Metal Company, but these findings were not released to the public until the summer of 1973. Did not the government have an obligation to release their findings as soon as they were known? Did not the public also have the right to be informed about the findings as soon as they were known?

• Given that the results of the provincial government's tests alarmed many people living near lead-smelting plants, would the government have been justified in not releasing any findings until it could determine with more certainty

-the source of the pollution?
-the dangers of lead pollution to human beings?

- In the case of the Canada Metal Company, was the government acting irresponsibly in releasing its first report on lead pollution before comparative tests had been undertaken in other areas of the city?

- Once the Ministry of the Environment's findings were made known, should people living near the Canada Metal Company have had their blood tested? Should these tests have been compulsory for everyone or should they have been voluntary?

- If the government had decided to undertake additional research before releasing any report, what obligation would it have had to safeguard the health of company workers and area residents while the research results were pending?

- Should the costs for these tests be paid for by
  -individual residents and workers affected?
  -the provincial government?
  -the City of Toronto
  -the company that was suspected of causing the pollution?

Should the costs have been shared by all or by some of the above? If so, by whom?

- Was the provincial government justified in ordering the closure of the Canada Metal Company?

or

- Should it have first tried to reduce the lead levels by requesting the company to install a filtering system before ordering a total shutdown of its operations?

- To what extent should the provincial government be held financially responsible for the loss of (a) wages to workers, (b) profits to the company suffered as a result of the closure?

- When it became clear in 1979 that the Canada Metal

Company's activities were still causing lead pollution in the environment because of poor maintenance procedures and the lack of back-up pollution control devices, was the provincial government justified in giving the company over a year in which to comply with the new pollution control order? Should not the company have been closed down until the 25 steps outlined by the government to control lead emissions had been completed?

Parallel Situation

Commercial and sports fishing on the English-Wabigoon River system in Northern Ontario was closed down by the provincial government in 1970 when dangerous mercury compounds caused by industrial waste were found in the system and the fish. As a result, the Indians of the White Dog and Grassy Narrows reserves, who earned their living through commercial fishing and working as fishing guides, were left without work. Few alternate employment opportunities were available to them. While the provincial government did provide welfare payments for the unemployed Indians, no serious attempt was made to clean up the river system or to develop other forms of employment. For years the Indians pleaded with the government to at least reopen the area for sports fishing so that they could resume work as guides. Finally, in 1978, the government announced plans for a limited reopening of the river system. The Indians were to be allowed to fish for carp which, though contaminated, would be processed into fertilizer oil at a plant in the United States. "We're fortunate to find an outlet for contaminated fish," declared Leo Bernier, Ontario's Northern Affairs minister. Unfortunately, however, few jobs would be created for Indians as a result of the government's plans.

Was the government justified in closing down the river system completely rather than leaving it open for sports fishing and posting a warning sign about the pollution?

- Should the government have shut down the industries causing the mercury pollution?

- Would the government have been justified in seeking compensation from the industries that were responsible for polluting the English-Wabigoon River system?

- Should the provincial government have paid compensation to the Indians who lost their jobs when the river system was closed down?

- Is the government responsible for developing new forms of employment for the Indians? Why? Why not?

- Should the government reopen the rivers to commercial fishing even though they are still polluted?

- Do you think that government plans to reopen the river system represent a *serious* attempt to provide employment for Indians? Should not the government also open its own oil-fertilizer plant near the reserves in order to provide more jobs for the native peoples?

Industrial Rights and Responsibilities

- Was the Canada Metal company justified in protesting the government's decision to close down its operations because
  - -leaded gasoline also results in lead pollution and the government did not ban the use of such gasoline?
  - -it has a long history of pollution control?
  - -it was willing to install new filtering devices?

- Should the company have been allowed to reopen before the new filtering system was installed or should it have remained closed until the system was operational even if this meant it would remain closed for several weeks?

- Should the company be made to install expensive equipment designed to (a) reduce, (b) eliminate lead pollution? If so, should the cost be paid for by
  - -the company?

-the provincial government?
-both the company and the government equally?

• To what extent was it the company's responsibility to install a back-up pollution control system long before it was finally ordered to do so by government order in 1979?

• From the evidence presented in this case, do you think that the Canada Metal Company should pay (a) all of, (b) part of the costs involved in
-testing the blood of company employees and nearby residents?
-medically treating any employees and residents found to have unacceptably high lead levels in their blood?
-relocating those families that were advised to move by medical officials?
-replacing the lead-contaminated soils in the surrounding area?

• In each of the following situations, to what extent should the company be held legally or morally responsible for the results of its business activities? Give reasons for your answers.
-A drug manufacturer creates a pill that results in physical and mental deformation of babies if it is taken by an expectant mother.
-A manufacturer produces cigarettes that have been shown to be related to the development of cancer in humans. What responsibility does the farmer who grows the tobacco bear?
-Fumes from an insecticide used to spray crops cause a serious blood disease in children playing in a nearby field.
-A hotel man continues to serve liquor to a man who is obviously intoxicated.
-A chemical fertilizer plant contaminates the atmosphere with an odor that is medically safe but ex-

tremely unpleasant to nearby residents.

- In May 1980 Dr. Gordon Atherley, president of the Canadian Centre for Occupational Health and Safety, estimated that there were some 10 000 Canadian workers suffering from job-related cancer, asbestosis, silicosis, and a host of other diseases. While labor leaders urge governments to enact strict health and safety regulations, employers argue for the replacement of government legislation with guidelines that will allow industry to regulate itself. Leaders of industry maintain that strict regulations are expensive to implement and lead to plant closures. Since the 1980 closing of the Bendix automotive plant in Windsor and the asbestos-making section of the Johns-Manville Plant in Metro Toronto (both of which had been proved to cause asbestos-related cancer in employees), many workers are nervously drawing the conclusion that insisting on safer working conditions could cost them their jobs.
  - Do you think that industry should be allowed to regulate its own health and safety standards?
  - In the event of a plant closure through inability to implement government imposed health and safety standards, should the government and/or the plant owners be responsible for providing alternative employment and/or compensation for the plant's employees?
  - Should industries be allowed to close rather than comply with government health and safety standards? Why? Why not?
  - Should the government pay (a) part (b) all of the cost involved in implementing health and safety standards imposed by government regulations? Why? Why not?

- To what extent do you believe that it is the responsibility of a company to protect people–employees and nearby residents–exposed to health hazards as a result of its operations?

Media Rights and Responsibility

Should the media—newspapers, radio, and television—have written reports on the *possible* dangers of lead pollution without first determining whether or not such dangers were a reality in this situation? Why? Why not?

In what sense, if any, would the media have been neglecting their duty if they had not reported the possible dangers of lead pollution?

Were the lead-smelting companies justified in seeking to stop the broadcasting of the CBC program "Dying of Lead" because it was biassed insofar as it documented a case against lead pollution?

Do you think that representatives from the lead-smelting companies should have been allowed to participate in the program to answer accusations concerning the incidence and effects of lead pollution? Should the CBC have allowed the lead-smelting industries to air their own program giving their side of the case?

Parallel Situation

The invention of the birth-control pill was hailed by many people as one of the greatest inventions of the twentieth century. Its use provided women, for the first time, with an acceptable and safe method of preventing unwanted pregnancies. Newspapers, radio, and television echoed medical experts in pointing out the benefits of the pill and advocating its use. By the mid 1970s, however, the media began giving widespread coverage to the possible ill effects of the pill. Women using it or contemplating its use learned that it could cause, among other things, heart attacks and blood clotting. Although the media reports were based on medical findings, many members of the medical profession objected to the media's coverage, claiming that it was biassed against the pill. Doctors pointed out that while some women might suffer ill effects from using the pill, this was certainly not true for all women. In attempting to warn women of possible dangers, the doctors accused the media of causing unnecessary alarm that would lead many females to stop taking the pill. And, according to a number of doctors, the health risk associated with pregnancy was far greater for women generally than were the health risks associated with the pill.

Are the media acting irresponsibly in reporting on the dangers of the pill? Would they be acting more responsibly if they did not report such dangers?

Should any newspaper, radio, and television report on the pill include equal information on both the advantages and disadvantages of using the pill?

Because of the present controversy surrounding the use of the pill, should the media refrain from making any comments on its advantages or disadvantages?

Assuming that women have the right to know the pros and cons of using the pill, how can they best be informed on this matter?

Is the media coverage of the possible ill effects resulting from the use of the pill any more or less justified than the media's coverage of the possible ill effects resulting from lead pollution?

Residents' Rights and Responsibilities

Did the people who lived near the Canada Metal Company have the right to demand that the plant be closed until

- -the provincial government was satisfied that the level of lead pollution in the area was reduced to an acceptable level?
- -medical evidence showed that no residents exhibited high levels of lead in their blood?

To what extent should parents be held responsible if their children contact lead poisoning as a result of eating lead-contaminated soil or any vegetation grown in such soil? Do parents have the same responsibility to ensure that children do not eat lead-contaminated paint?

• In each of the following situations should the parents be held responsible for what happens to their child? Give reasons for your answers.

- A seven-year-old boy, who has been told not to play on the road, decides to use his skateboard, a birthday present from his parents, on the road. He is hit by a car and seriously injured.
- A ten-year-old girl picks up her father's hunting rifle, not knowing it is loaded, and accidentally shoots and kills her six-year-old brother.
- A four-year-old girl climbs on top of a kitchen counter, opens a cupboard and drinks some poisonous household cleanser she finds there. She becomes severely mentally retarded as a result.

Doctors' Rights and Responsibilities

• Did the City of Toronto medical authorities have a moral responsibility to demand that all nearby residents of the Canada Metal Company be tested to determine whether or not they were suffering from any form of lead pollution?

• When it was discovered that some children did have excessively high blood lead levels, were the medical authorities fulfilling their obligations by simply advising the families to move away from the area, or should they have demanded that the government close the Canada Metal Company until satisfactory pollution controls had been installed?

• What responsibility do doctors have to prevent as well as to cure illness? Does this mean that they should have a legal right to ensure that known causes of medical problems, such as alcohol, cigarettes, and pollution are eliminated from our society?

The Public Hearing on Lead Pollution

- Do you agree with the government's decision to hold a public hearing on lead pollution at which both the lead-smelting companies and those opposing their operations could present their arguments?
- Do not such hearings inevitably favor large companies because they have the financial resources to pay for research to support their case and to bring in expert witnesses to testify on their behalf?
- In order to allow the general public the same opportunities as the lead-smelting companies, should the government have provided money for individuals and groups of individuals to present a case against lead smelting operations?
- Were the findings of the public hearing satisfactory, in your opinion? Why? Why not?
- Do you believe that the recommendations made as a result of the public hearing were sufficient to minimize any threat to public health caused by the presence of the lead-smelting companies in residential areas?
- What additional recommendations, if any, would you have liked?

Summary Questions

- Given the uncertainties surrounding both the amount of pollution that is harmful to health and the present and future medical and psychological effects of pollution on human beings, should not the government severely restrict the activities of all industries suspected of polluting the environment?
- When government attempts to have the lead-smelting companies pay for replacing the lead-contaminated soils failed, profits from the provincial lottery scheme were used to pay for the cleanup. Was this a good use of provincial lottery profits? Should the government have

ordered the companies to pay all of the cost involved rather than accepting only a one-third contribution?

Given the history of the Canada Metal Company's response to provincial government orders to control lead-pollution, do you agree with the City of Toronto's 1980 decision to build an apartment complex on land near the lead-smelting plant? To what extent is your answer influenced by the fact that the apartment complex is designed to house low, rather than middle or high-income tenants?

Research Activities

• Examine the provisions of Ontario's Environmental Act relating to industrial pollution. Do you think these provisions are sufficient to protect the health of the public? Do they represent an unfair burden on industrial companies? What changes, if any, would you like to see in the Act?

• Examine the provisions of Ontario's 1979 Occupational Health and Safety Act. Are these provisions strict enough to protect the health and safety of workers? Do they represent an unfair burden on industrial companies? What changes, if any, would you like to see in this Act?

3 COMMUNITY PRESERVATION

Trefann Court I

On 10 February 1966, the *Globe and Mail* reported Toronto City Council's approval of an urban renewal plan for Trefann Court. The report, brief but to the point, was on one of the newspaper's inside pages. Trefann Court was described as "a rundown 24-acre industrial, residential, and commercial area" located a short distance east of the commercial and retail centre of downtown Toronto. The urban renewal plan, the report noted, called for "the clearance of 16 acres, and would require the demolition of 255 existing housing units occupied by 1,000 persons. Nine acres of the cleared land would be used for a 250-unit public housing project to accommodate 1,100 persons. Seven acres would be resold for industrial use." According to the report, the city council expected to be able to begin work on the plan within four months. The newspaper reported that the cost of the plan would be $9,144,000 and that "the average family income in the Trefann Court area is about $3,600."

Pre-Urban Renewal: 1934 to 1966

The plan came as no surprise to the residents of the area.

As early as 1934 Trefann Court had been identified, along with areas to its north, south, east, and west, as a "slum" that should be torn down and rebuilt. In that year–the hundredth anniversary of the founding of the City of Toronto–the lieutenant-governor of Ontario, Dr. Herbert A. Bruce, chaired a special committee of enquiry that was established to examine housing conditions in the city. The resulting document, known as the Bruce Report, focussed on an area commonly referred to as Cabbagetown. The name Cabbagetown derived from the fact that the area's original Irish residents planted cabbages in their front yards at the turn of the century. Trefann Court was, in fact, only one part of Cabbagetown and it was named after a street of the same name that was located in its midst. The Bruce Report surveyed over 3000 houses in the whole Cabbagetown area. Of these it reported that 40 percent did not meet minimum health standards; 9 percent had no indoor toilets, 27 percent had no bathrooms, and 45 percent had no central heating. Based on its findings, the report recommended that the city undertake a mammoth slum clearance in the area and that both the provincial and federal governments be asked to provide money to replace the existing houses with low-rental housing.

No action was taken on the Bruce Report's recommendations until the late 1940s and 1950s. During this period virtually all of the housing in Cabbagetown, with the exception of that in the Trefann Court area, was demolished and replaced by large public housing developments. Although no official urban renewal plan was approved for Trefann Court throughout this period, most of the area's residents recognized that it was only a matter of time before their houses would also be demolished and public housing units built in their place. When the city finally announced its plan for the area in 1966, the uncertainty that had faced the residents for the preceding twenty years finally became a reality.

Trefann Court in 1966

Little had changed in Trefann Court during these years. If anything, the quality of housing had deteriorated even more. Landlords, knowing that the city intended at some point to tear down the area's houses, had long ceased to make any but the most necessary repairs to their properties. And in some cases even these were neglected: most of the rented properties had broken windows, plaster falling off the walls, and inadequate plumbing. As one landlord said "Well, why should I put a lot of money into these homes if they are going to be expropriated?" Some homeowners had found the uncertainty of waiting for the city to act too much and had sold their homes and moved away from the area. Such homeowners frequently ended up receiving less for their houses than they were worth simply because few people wanted to buy homes in an area that would eventually be demolished. Others had tried to sell their homes but either could not find buyers or could not afford to move to new homes with the money they were offered. So they stayed put.

For those who remained in 1966, the Trefann Court area represented a five-block section of the city surrounded by massive public housing developments. The housing contained within this area varied from small, cramped, and drab frame cottages based on the prize-winning design for a workman's cottage at the Crystal Palace Exhibition in London, England (1851), to classic, solid three-storey brick houses with verandas and ornate cornices. Sprinkled among the houses were three auto-wreckers, three garages, an overnight hostel for homeless single men, a hotel, a small furniture factory, two warehouses, and a number of small stores, businesses, and restaurants.

Although the area's residents were predominantly of English descent, almost 40 percent came from such countries as Greece, Poland, Germany, Portugal, and

Bulgaria. In 1966 the total number of people living in the area was 1215. About 30 percent of these owned their own homes, while about 70 percent were tenants living in rental accommodation. The number of homeowners had decreased over the previous ten years as those who could sell their homes had moved. Many of these homes had been bought cheaply by absentee landlords who rented out rooms or flats to tenants. Single lodgers and childless couples accounted for over 40 percent of the area's residents. Less than half of the people living in Trefann Court were employed; the rest were either unemployed, retired, or living on some form of welfare.

At first the news that the city finally had approved an urban renewal plan for the area was greeted with relief by a number of the residents. Many homeowners, who had been unable to sell their homes privately because of the uncertainty of the city's plan for the area, were pleased that at last the plan was settled and that the city would buy their homes from them and tear them down. Many tenants were initially pleased with the plan because the city promised them priority in renting houses and apartments in the new public housing units to be built in the area. However, the area's residents were soon beset by misgivings. Homeowners realized that the amount the city was prepared to pay for their homes was insufficient to buy similar homes in other parts of the city. Tenants discovered that there were few, if any, places they could move to while the new public housing units were being built.

Negotiating Compensation for Homeowners and Tenants
The city recognized these problems and hired a community officer, Marjaleena Repo, to assist residents with their relocation problems. The community worker's presence served, however, to focus people's attention on the enormity of the problem facing them. Shortly

after her appointment, Ms. Repo became convinced that the plan for the area was more likely to hurt people than to help them. There were, she was convinced, few places where people could relocate. She began urging people in the neighborhood to get together to discuss what should be done. Her efforts coincided with the residents' rapidly growing disillusionment with the city's plan. Very soon a Trefann Court Residents' Association (TCRA) was formed. The TCRA consisted of tenants and homeowners, united by one common aim: to ensure that suitable alternative accommodation would be available for everyone forced to leave the area because of the urban renewal plan.

At first the Association decided to make sure that the city paid fair prices to homeowners for their properties. The city had already made a number of offers but the prices were too low to allow homeowners to buy another home elsewhere—and few were in a position to take on large new mortgages. Area residents became further angered when they discovered that the city had budgeted an average of $9800 per house, although city officials estimated that the real "market value" of the houses, if they were sold privately, was an average of $13 400. There appeared little that the residents could do. If they refused to sell their homes to the city for the price offered, the city had the power to expropriate the homes from the owners for the same price. Their only hope was to negotiate with the city to increase the payment for their houses. In order to help with these negotiations, the TCRA decided to hire "the best possible legal expert" to represent them. Each homeowner contributed $10 to hire a lawyer and a total of $600 was raised.

On 28 September and 19 October 1966, lawyers who were experienced in defending expropriated homeowners from other urban renewal areas appeared before city council and requested that the city continue to negotiate with homeowners rather than expropriate their properties at low prices. One of the lawyers, James McCallum, pointed out that some of his clients had mortgages on their homes that were worth more than the total amount the city was prepared to pay for the properties themselves. He cited one example of a house that had been sold for $8500 cash and later the same day resold to another man for $500 down and $13 000 in mortgages. As the city was now offering this homeowner only $8500 for his house, Mr. McCallum noted, this meant that "the man goes away from the property with no roof over his head and still [owing] $5,000 in cash."

The city's reaction to such situations was not sympathetic. William Callow, the city solicitor, responded by saying: "It's not our job to get them off the hook because they signed an over-valued mortgage." Finally, however, the city politicians did agree that they would continue to negotiate with homeowners until February 1967. If by that time some homeowners had still not sold their properties to the city, then negotiations would cease and the properties would be expropriated.

Although the TCRA had won in one sense, insofar as the city had committed itself to continue negotiations with homeowners, there was little feeling of victory among the members. Homeowners were becoming increasingly concerned that even if the city was to pay them the real "market value" for their homes, rather than the original lower prices they had been offered, they still would not receive enough to buy another home elsewhere. The market value of a house is the price it would fetch if it were sold privately rather than to the city. But in areas such as Trefann Court that had been designated for urban renewal, it was extremely difficult to establish true market values. The homes could not be sold privately; the city required them to make way for the new developments. For this reason, property owners in the Trefann area felt that they could not receive a fair price for their homes. As a result they decided that, rather than true market value which they believed was impossible to determine, the city should pay them "replacement value." This meant that homeowners should receive enough to allow them to purchase another home. In addition to this demand the area residents, both homeowners and tenants, asked the city to pay the various costs, such as moving, involved in relocating.

The city responded by flatly refusing to pay such costs and by pointing out that it could not guarantee residents replacement value for the homes. As the mayor of Toronto, Philip Givens, pointed out, there was only a certain amount of money available to finance the whole urban renewal scheme and this had to be used for purchasing properties, demolition, and building the new developments. The federal government provided 50 percent, the provincial government 25 percent, and Metropolitan Toronto 25 percent. Mayor Givens made it clear that this involvement of three levels of government in the process meant that no one level–especially Metro, which was contributing the least to the overall cost–had the authority to decide to pay replacement values for properties. Such decisions, he said, had to be agreed to by all the government authorities involved. And the federal government, because it was providing the largest share of the money, would have the most say as to how much money should be spent for purchasing homes.

Residents' Opposition to Urban Renewal Is Solidified

Convinced that the funds available for urban renewal would not be increased by any of the governments, residents of Trefann Court saw that they would not receive replacement value for their homes. This led them to question why, if they could not afford to buy homes elsewhere, they had to move at all. In addition, now that they were faced with the threat of having to leave their homes and their neighborhood, many residents began openly to voice their objections to the kind of changes urban renewal would bring to the Trefann area. Meetings of TCRA had brought together people who had lived in the area for many years. Coming together to discuss their common problems had helped them to appreciate the good things about their community: the fact that many of the homes, though in need of repair, were basically good, solid homes; the fact that families had lived in the neighborhood for years and knew one another well. It was not simply the fact that their homes were to be torn down by the city that concerned the area's residents, but also that their community–their whole way of life–was to be destroyed. And this, the members of the TCRA decided, was something that the politicians must be made to understand. Their feelings were summed up in a comment written in the association's newsletter that was now being distributed to all residents in order to keep them informed about what was happening in their neighborhood:

> Since when has the city come to the people and asked them any questions, listened to their ideas, or consulted them as to what is needed or desired in the area slated for redevelopment? . . . When are our "highly qualified" and "professional" city planners going to realize that we are fellow human beings, that we have families and children whom we care for, that we have a way of life that we value, that the majority of us like the area and would have wanted to see it improved rather than torn down? Instead the planners and politicians treat us as if we were children or idiots or scum (they call us "slum dwellers" to justify their highhanded methods) and our opinions and feelings are worth nothing at all.

Clearly, the people of Trefann Court were now seriously questioning the whole basis of urban renewal planning. Once these questions were voiced, TCRA agreed to stop fighting for fair prices for homeowners and instead to concentrate on opposing the whole plan for urban renewal in their area. A brief was presented by the TCRA to city council in November 1966. The brief requested that the city scrap the urban renewal plan for the area and replace it with a new plan that would allow most of the existing buildings to remain and to be rehabilitated and renovated. In this way, the brief's supporters argued, a majority of homes could be saved and only those that were in such bad shape that they were not worth putting money into would need to be demolished. This alternative plan, the supporters also suggested, would cost considerably less than the estimated nine million dollars needed to implement the city's plan. The city rejected the brief. As one newspaper—the *Globe and Mail*—was to report, city politicians were "shocked into silence" at the idea that people in Trefann Court would "rather live in their near-slum neighborhood than accept the city's plan for urban renewal."

While the city refused to drop the official plan, the legal status of the same plan became questionable. The plan, though approved by city officials, had never been approved by the Ontario Municipal Board (OMB). Such approval was necessary for any city plans that involved major expenditures and required zoning changes in order to be implemented. The Trefann Court plan not only involved such major expenditures but it also necessitated zoning changes because the area, as it was presently zoned, did not allow for the high-rise public housing developments that were proposed.

On 1 January 1967 a reorganization of the Metropolitan Toronto system of government came into effect when the thirteen municipalities under its authority were reduced to five. Because of this change, the OMB decided that any plans, such as the Trefann Court one, that had not received OMB approval prior to Metro's reorganization, must go back for a second approval to the municipal council from which it came. Consequently, the Trefann Court urban renewal plan was no longer a legal plan until the city formally approved it a second time. For almost two years from that date the city refused either to approve the plan again or to replace it with a new one.

The reason for the city's lack of action was due in no small part to city officials' desire to gain approval for the plan from the Trefann Court residents before resubmitting it for OMB approval. They hoped that if the people were to accept the plan, the opposition would fade and the chances of successfully implementing it would increase. With this in mind, city politicians began attending TRCA meetings to explain the plan to people and to emphasize its benefits. City planners also participated in these meetings. Both the politicians and the planners argued that most of the area was in such bad shape that the only way of improving it was to "tear it down and rebuild it." Then, instead of slum conditions, there would be modern, clean, low-rental housing units. The residents were unimpressed by these arguments. They replied by showing what had happened in surrounding areas that had undergone similar renewal–large public housing units replacing single-family homes. While they agreed that many homes had been in bad condition, the Trefann area residents felt that the high-rise buildings had replaced homes but not the sense of community that had once existed in these areas. People living in these buildings did not know their neighbors in the same way as people living in houses did, they pointed out. And crime rates and acts of violence had increased because people no longer had a feeling of pride that comes with a sense of belonging to a community. Having witnessed these effects of urban renewal in surrounding areas, there was little that the politicians or planners could say that would persuade Trefann residents that it was in their best interests to replace their run-down homes with sparkling new high-rises.

The Issues I

Rights of Residents vs. the Power of Government

- Do you believe that in 1966, Trefann Court, with its run-down homes and stores, auto wrecking yards, hostel for homeless men, and so on, was a blighted area that represented a threat to a healthy city?

- In a run-down area such as Trefann Court, should the primary responsibility for bringing about change rest with the residents? If they fail to do so, should the responsibility then rest with the local authority?

- Does the fact that some Trefann homeowners, especially the absentee landlords, had allowed their properties to deteriorate take away the right of the area's residents to have this responsibility? If so, does this not penalize those residents who have maintained their properties?

- Given the conditions of the time, was not the Trefann Court urban renewal plan, approved by the City of Toronto in 1966, calling for the clearance of 255 houses and the building of new high-rise public housing developments, a reasonable response to the situation?

- Should the city have spoken to the residents to find out their opinions before drawing up the plan? Should the city have circulated copies of the plan to all residents before the council was asked to approve it? Was there anything else the city should have done? If so, what and why?

- Would the city have been any more or less justified in passing a plan that called for the total demolition of the Trefann area in order to build a large public park? Why?

- Would the local authority have been justified if it had expropriated part of the area's land in order to build
    - -a local hospital?
    - -a public school?
    - -a major expressway?

-a profitable factory employing many people?
-a parking lot for an apartment complex?
-an urgently needed firehall?
-a bowling alley?

• In each of the above cases give reasons for your answers. Would it make any difference if the land was occupied by (a) a profitable fruit farm, (b) working-class homes, (c) middle-class homes, (d) factories, (e) shops, (f) offices? When should expropriation be allowed?

• Do you believe that democratically elected governments, whether at the local, provincial, or federal level, have the right to pass laws that will change how and where people live?

Citizens' Responses

Were the residents of Trefann Court justified in opposing the 1966 plan for urban renewal in their neighborhood?

• Should the city have hired a community officer to help residents with their relocation plans? Once it did, did this make their opposition less justifiable?

• If the city had provided the residents with equivalent housing (a) in a downtown working-class neighborhood 5 miles [8 km] away, (b) in a distant suburb 12 miles [19.2 km] away, would their opposition be less justifiable?

• Should the plan have been withdrawn because of the homeowners right to live in an area of their choice? Should tenants have the same rights as homeowners? Should transients have the same rights as homeowners and tenants? Should absentee landlords have the same rights as homeowners and tenants?

• Should government policy be such that if there is general opposition to a plan by an area's residents, including both homeowners and tenants, then the plan will be withdrawn?

• In each of the following situations should opposition from (a) homeowners, (b) tenants, be grounds for scrapping the plans:

-a local authority plan to build (i) a public housing development for 100 people, (ii) less expensive but not public housing, on land in the midst of a community of very expensive private homes?

-a developer's plan to erect a 20-storey office building on land adjacent to single-family homes?

Parallel Situation

In recent years some city governments have enacted legislation allowing group homes for the mentally and physically handicapped, emotionally disturbed children, alcoholics, and former prisoners to locate in residential areas. Supporters of group homes claim that treatment for disability or rehabilitation into society can best be carried out in such homes where the residents live in a family atmosphere and can achieve more independence than is normally associated with living in large, impersonal institutions. Many residential neighborhoods, however, are extremely reluctant to have group homes in their areas, claiming that they will result in a lowering of property values. In particular, residential groups are opposed to having homes for alcoholics and former prisoners in their midst because they feel these "undesirable" people are dangerous and should not be allowed to live alongside ordinary families.

• Should cities permit group homes to be located in residential areas?

• Should local opposition be sufficient to bring about the withdrawal of plans for a group home designed to house

-the mentally handicapped?

-the physically handicapped?

-emotionally disturbed children?

-alcoholics?
-former prisoners?

In each case state why you think the local authority should agree or not to withdraw its plan for a group home.

- If cities allow group homes in residential areas, should they be responsible for ensuring that such homes are well run and properly staffed?
- Should a group home for alcoholics be allowed in an area where most of the families have young children?
- Should there be any kind of restrictions on the type of group homes that can locate in residential areas? What sort of restrictions would you suggest and why?
- What similarities are there between a neighborhood's opposition to the location of a group home in its area and the Trefann residents' opposition to the city's original plan for urban renewal in their area? Are both types of opposition equally justified? If not, why not?

Research Activity

Find out if group homes are allowed in your community (this information can be obtained from your local authority's planning office). Are there any limitations on the type of homes that are permitted? What other regulations, if any, are there controlling the establishment and the functioning of such homes? What additional regulations would you like to see and why?

Trefann Court II

The Split between Trefann Homeowners and Tenants

Homeowners in Trefann were, as a group, more strongly opposed than the tenants to the urban renewal plan for tearing down homes and replacing them with high-rises. Rather than approving the existing plan, homeowners wanted money to renovate their existing homes. The tenants, however, did not support the homeowners' demands. They feared that if the homes, rooms, or apartments they rented were to be renovated, their landlords would then be able to charge higher rents than they could afford. Many tenants thought they would be better off living in the public-housing units that the city wanted to build in the area. At least in such buildings the amount of rent they paid would depend on the amount of money they had. As TCRA had both homeowners and tenants among its members, this difference in attitude towards the plan eventually caused a major split in the association. The tenants, feeling that their interests would not be served unless some form of urban renewal occurred, became reluctant to work with the homeowners, who were united in their insistence that urban renewal, as it was defined by the city, should not take place.

These differences also led to general feelings of antagonism and mistrust between the tenants and the homeowners. The tensions that resulted came to a head in January 1968. A tenant in one of the homes in the area complained to another tenant member of the TCRA (a Mrs. Pat Rice) that her house was so cold that her children had to sleep wearing their snowsuits. Mrs. Rice brought the situation up at a meeting of the TCRA. There was a general discussion about the bad state of many of the rented homes, including the fact that many such homes lacked adequate heating. The landlords of these places, the majority of whom did not live in the area, obviously were not interested in paying to keep their houses in a state of repair when they believed that before long the city would buy their properties and tear them down. The TCRA decided that one way of tackling this problem would be to take temperatures in various rooms in a number of rented houses over a two-week period. Then, when it was established (as they expected) that temperatures were well below those that the city required landlords to provide by law, they would present their evidence to the city. In this way, TCRA argued, they could attack the city for allowing landlords to break the law by not heating their properties sufficiently. All members of TCRA present at the meeting agreed upon this plan of action.

A few days later, however, after a night when the temperature had dropped well below zero in Toronto, the *Globe and Mail* ran a large front-page photograph of four bewildered children lying huddled together on a bed, wearing snowsuits, in a room of a house in the Trefann area. The accompanying article said the temperature inside the house was -1 degree Centigrade. It also pointed out that the reason for the low temperature was not inadequate heating but no heating at all, because the gas had been turned off when previous heating bills were unpaid.

Reaction to the article was varied. Newspaper reporters and television cameramen descended on the area to take pictures. Stories of the plight of many of the Trefann area residents brought food parcels and cheques from residents in wealthy areas of the city. Members of TCRA reacted angrily. They were annoyed that their agreed-upon plan of action to get the city to do something about the inadequate heating in many of the area's homes had been thwarted. They felt that they had been deceived by Mrs. Rice who—though she had agreed to the plan—had, they discovered, contacted the newspaper that had run the picture and article concerning the freezing children. The fact that the lack of heating was found to be the result of unpaid bills, rather than an uncaring landlord, made them particularly angry because they felt they had been misled. It further served to reinforce an opinion that many homeowners had of tenants, namely, that most of them were on welfare and spent their money on liquor instead of paying their bills. But what angered TCRA most of all was the kind of publicity that their neighborhood received as a result of the incident. This publicity appeared to confirm what city officials had been saying all along and what TCRA had been denying: that the area was a slum and should be torn down.

It was not the first time that Trefann Court residents were to express resentment of the way their neighborhood was described by the media. Newspaper photographs and stories and television reports all seemed, in the TCRA's opinion, to dwell on the poor conditions present in the area's homes. No attention was paid to the well-kept homes. A typical report that backed up TCRA's opinion appeared in the *Toronto Telegram*: "The first thing that hits you when you walk into most homes in the Trefann Court area is the stench," wrote a reporter. He continued: "It's bad, unbelievably bad in many cases . . . greasy food odours, week-old garbage." Most of the houses were, according to this reporter's observations, "filthy," and presented major fire hazards because of faulty wiring, the use of small coal or wood stoves to heat them, and a total lack of ventilation. The tenants in these homes, the reporter concluded, despaired of ever having decent accommodation and looked "old beyond their years." Similar articles and newspaper editorials describing much of the area's housing as being "unfit for human habitation" did little to support the TCRA's argument that the area was worth saving.

The split between the tenants and the homeowners that came to a head over the "cold houses" situation became permanent soon after. Tenants withdrew from the TCRA and formed their own association, the Trefann Neighbors and Tenants Association (TNT). They were joined by some property owners, most of whom were landlords who wanted the city to go ahead with the urban renewal plan so that they could then sell their run-down properties for demolition. As the TNT was formed to urge the city to proceed with urban renewal so that public housing units would be built for them, the landlords obviously had more in common with this group than they did with the TCRA, which was totally opposed to any urban renewal scheme that meant demolishing homes.

The Issues II

The Media

• Did the media have a right to print and televise stories about the poor housing conditions in Trefann Court?

• Given the state of some of the houses in Trefann, did not the media have a responsibility to publicize the kind of conditions that existed there?

• Did the newspaper stories and photographs and the television reports on conditions in Trefann violate the residents' right to privacy? How? If so, would this also apply to absentee landlords? Why? Why not?

• What responsibility did the media have to inform the public about the more favorable aspects of Trefann Court?

• Do the media have a right to expose the real facts that are involved in a controversial issue? Why? Why not?

• Do they have a right to openly campaign for and against certain public projects? Why? Why not?

• In your opinion, was the newspaper acting responsibly when it ran the story about the freezing temperatures inside one Trefann house?

• Does the media have the right to report on any story that they consider to be of importance to the lives of the community? What limitations, if any, should there be?

• Should the media have a right to report on
-a housing area where an epidemic is taking place

even though such reports may frighten and alarm many people?

-the private lives of public figures?

-the private lives of private figures?

Trefann Court III

A State of Limbo: 1968 to 1970

For over two years the members of TCRA and TNT met separately and worked separately to achieve what seemed to be their opposing aims. City officials tried to work with both groups, hoping that if their differences could be resolved, a plan agreed upon by everyone could be adopted for the area. When the city agreed, at the urging of TNT members, to acquire some of the worst properties in the neighborhood and tear them down, members of TCRA objected that, lacking an official plan for the area, the city had no power to do this. The city pointed out that the properties in question had been abandoned, were overrun with rats, and posed a serious health threat to people living nearby. The houses were in such bad shape that they could fall down and seriously injure or kill young children who were continually playing near them. Still TCRA refused to agree to demolition. Instead, they accused city officials of deliberately causing the properties to fall into disrepair by repeatedly refusing to enforce minimum housing standards. It was, members of TCRA claimed, a deliberate plan on the part of the city to ignore houses clearly in violation of the city's own health and physical safety requirements in the hope that, once these houses were badly deteriorated, there would be no alternative other than to tear them down.

Finally the city wrote the provincial and federal governments asking if they could acquire the properties and tear them down even though there was no official plan for the area. The city also requested the two levels of government to share the costs involved. The province replied that no action could be taken by the city until it had an officially approved plan and that the residents of the area must agree to the plan before the provincial government would consider sharing the cost of any form of urban renewal in Trefann. The response from the federal government was the same.

Before the city could get such agreement for a plan, the federal government announced, in late 1968, that all funds for urban renewal were to be frozen while a Federal Task Force on Housing and Urban Development worked out a reassessment of housing policy in Canada. Two days later Metro Toronto's funds for urban renewal were cut out of the budget by Metro politicians. At the same time, Metro agreed to keep one million dollars in the budget to pay for a new zoo that was planned. This decision caused members of TNT to comment angrily: "Let us live in the nice new zoo and move the animals to Trefann."

The Federal Task Force report was released in January 1969. Its contents particularly pleased members of the TCRA. Traditional methods of urban renewal were criticized in the report. Designating an area for such renewal frequently created slums, the report suggested, by causing property owners—especially landlords—in such areas to neglect the upkeep of their properties. And, the report noted, tearing down houses and replacing them with high-rise public housing units was not the answer to poor housing conditions because such developments often resulted in more problems than they solved. A better alternative, the report concluded, was to encourage, where possible, the upgrading of older homes in rundown sections of cities and the building of low-rise subsidized housing units to replace houses that were beyond renovation. The TCRA's initial pleasure with the task force report quickly evaporated when it became clear that the federal government was not going to act on its recommendations and the cabinet minister who had headed the task force, Paul Hellyer, resigned from the government.

Homeowners and Tenants Establish Urban Renewal Proposals

With federal funds for urban renewal frozen and the task force's recommendations apparently rejected, TCRA, TNT, and city council despaired of Trefann Court ever being improved. Then suddenly hope was revived when the federal government announced in January 1970 that it would spend up to four million dollars on urban renewal in Toronto. Both the Trefann Court associations realized that if their area was to get any of this money they would have to settle their differences and come up with a mutually agreed-upon set of proposals for urban renewal.

This is what they did. The proposals represented a compromise aimed at guaranteeing and protecting the rights of both homeowners and tenants. TCRA members agreed to the demolition of the worst run-down properties in the area, while TNT members agreed that only a limited amount of demolition and rebuilding should occur. The basic proposals were:

(1) No homeowner who wished to remain in Tefann Court would have to move. All homeowners, whether resident or absentee [landlords] who did not wish to sell their properties to the city would undertake necessary repairs to their properties so that they met the city's housing standards.

(2) If the city purchased properties which were part of a row and the other homeowners did not want to sell, thus making demolition impossible, the city would make necessary repairs to these properties so that they met the housing standards.

(3) Priority would be given to any resident of the area to rent or buy any housing unit purchased and repaired

by the city, as well as such units as might be built as a result of urban renewal. The rents and purchase prices of such properties were to be subsidized where necessary. Tenants were also to be provided with alternative accommodation if they had to move because of the plan and they were to be compensated for all moving costs.

Other proposals were directed towards defining the kind of urban renewal that should take place in Trefann Court. From these it was clearly apparent that none of the area's residents wanted to drastically alter their neighborhood. They did not want all the commerce and industry removed from the area but wanted instead to retain the residential/industrial nature of Trefann. Only those industries that were described as being "obnoxious or nuisances in the area" (such as the auto-wreckers) were to be moved. To further improve the appearance of the Trefann community, the city was requested to carry out an "improvement program of public works" that included such things as street repairs, providing better garbage pick-up, increasing parking space, and so on. Both tenants and homeowners also proposed that the city establish a community centre with social services and recreational facilities in the hostel for single men that existed in the area. This latter proposal, members of TCRA and TNT argued, would fulfil two objectives–it would provide much-needed recreational facilities for residents and would rid the area of the "shabby vacant-eyed male transients" who used the hostel. For years the presence of this hostel for transient men had been a constant source of irritation for families with children who lived nearby.

The proposals for urban renewal in Trefann did not deal only with the kind of renewal that was wanted, but also with how such renewal was to be planned. It was suggested that a "working committee" be set up to formulate an official plan for the area. This committee was to consist of representatives of all homeowners, tenants, and businessmen who wished to stay in the area. A planner who was acceptable to the working committee was to be hired by the city to work out the details of the plan with the committee. By insisting that the planner be "acceptable" to the working committee, the Trefann residents wanted to ensure that the person hired for the job would be sympathetic to their proposals for improving the area.

In summary, the series of proposals agreed to by TCRA and TNT was intended to provide for the full participation of the area's residents in designing a plan of urban renewal for Trefann. Such a plan would not change the basic nature of the community. As one resident put it: "We don't want Trefann Court to be pretty. It's a mixed-use area. . . . We don't mind industries. We like the area the way it is. There are some problems—there is some bad housing that should be cleared up and the auto-wreckers are a problem—but basically we like it the way it is."

Similar sentiments were expressed by other residents, many of whom feared that if Trefann Court were to become "pretty," middle-class people would be attracted to the area, start buying up homes and renovating them into fashionable "townhouses." This "invasion by the middle classes" into run-down parts of the city was becoming commonplace, especially in neighborhoods to the north of Trefann Court. Although the outward appearance of such areas was improved, this type of activity forced up the price of homes. Consequently, the amount of housing available for lower-income people was severely reduced. These people could not afford the higher prices asked for the homes and the tenants frequently found themselves without accommodation when landlords sold their properties to middle-class buyers who wanted to renovate them and turn them into single-family houses for themselves. Trefann Court residents were determined that this should not occur in their neighborhood. Their proposals for renewal were not, therefore, designed to make the area "pretty," but rather to ensure that a decent living environment was provided for the kind of people who had always lived there–the working class.

Once TCRA and TNT had agreed upon their proposals for Trefann, they submitted them to city council for adoption. Council members were both relieved and surprised that the tenants and homeowners of Trefann had been able to settle their differences and draw up a mutually acceptable set of proposals. On 4 March 1970, city council voted to make Trefann Court the city's priority area for urban renewal. The idea of a working committee to draw up the official renewal plan was favorably received by the council and it was agreed that representatives of both Trefann associations, together with select city aldermen, should serve on this committee. At the same time, the two associations' other proposals concerning the type of renewal that should take place were subjected to considerable debate. Many council members felt that they should not tie themselves down to such specific proposals before an official plan was designed; other council members, who supported the TCRA and TNT proposals, argued that the city should commit itself to the proposals "as a basis for urban renewal in Trefann." Eventually a compromise was reached whereby city council agreed that the proposals would be "taken into consideration" in designing the official Trefann renewal plan.

The Issues III

Neighborhood Development

• Should community groups have the right to control the kind of development that occurs in their neighborhood? Should there be any restrictions on this right? If so, what should they be?

• Do you agree with the Trefann residents' refusal to accept living in high-rise apartment buildings, because they believed such buildings lack a sense of community and warmth, is justified? Would this be sufficient reason to scrap any high-rise housing projects proposed for the Trefann area?

• Should families with young children live in high-rise buildings? Do you believe any unnecessary difficulties are caused by children living in such buildings? What restrictions, if any, should exist on the sale or rental of high-rise apartments to families with young children? Should governments provide support, where necessary, so that families with young children can live in single-family homes?

• Given the heavy demand for reasonably priced accommodation and the shortage of land in most cities, can the development of high-rise residential buildings be avoided? What alternatives are there?

• Do people with limited financial means have the right to expect to be provided with the reasonable housing of their choice? If so, how would you define reasonable?

• It has been suggested that all public housing should be phased out and replaced with a federal government shelter allowance paid to people judged needy by Ottawa. These low-income people would then be left to find the best housing they could in a totally private market. Do you agree with this suggestion? Should governments at any level–local, provincial, or federal–be involved in building housing for low-income people?

Research Activity

Find out if there is a local ratepayers' association in your area (most local authorities have lists of such associations). Contact the association and ask what say, if any, it has in controlling local development. Is it always informed about all developments that are planned for the area? Has it ever tried to have a development plan altered or withdrawn? If so, for what reasons and was it successful? Do the members of the association feel that they have sufficient power to control development, both small and large scale, in the area? What additional powers, if any, do they think they should have? Why?

Trefann Court IV

The Joint City/Trefann Residents Working Committee
Disappointed at the city's decision not to commit itself publicly to their proposals, members of TCRA and TNT were at first hesitant to appoint representatives to the working committee. They simply did not want to participate in the working committee until the city made a more solid commitment to their proposals. Only after the city-appointed chairman of the working committee, Alderman David Crombie, privately assured members of TCRA and TNT that he, personally, accepted their proposals as a minimum for urban renewal in Trefann, did the two associations agree to appoint representatives to the working committee.

Once the committee, consisting of Trefann homeowners, tenants, and businessmen, plus five city aldermen, was appointed, the first item of business concerned the hiring of a planner. The candidate selected for the job was Howard Cohen, a young Winnipeg architect. This appointment was approved after a small group of the Trefann area representatives on the working committee, together with officials from the City Planning Department, had interviewed a number of candidates for the job. Of all the applicants, Cohen was chosen because the working committee representatives thought he was most likely to be sympathetic to their ideas for improving the Trefann area. "It seemed like he was open," one of the committee members recollected later. "He was obviously bright and it seemed as if he was willing to listen and try things, and dig into the problems. He was the obvious choice."

Although members of the working committee were unanimous in their approval of Howard Cohen as planner, other items of business met with less agreement. In total, the working committee met 32 times over a period of 18 months before agreement was reached on an official plan for the Trefann area. Throughout this time it was obvious that members of TCRA and TNT still distrusted each other. While representatives of homeowners wanted a plan to allow the renovation of their homes, tenants pushed for a plan to allow the building of new rental accommodation. These differing objectives resulted in tensions and fights. At one point, TCRA representatives threatened to resign from the working committee when the city acquired a number of houses for demolition. TNT representatives, however, backed the city's action and eventually the homeowners withdrew their threatened resignations.

One thing both groups did agree upon was the need for a social survey of all area residents in order to find out what kind of housing and other facilities the people really wanted. The results of this survey showed that no one wanted the Trefann area to be drastically changed. While most people agreed that there were certain houses in such disrepair that they had to be demolished, no one wanted them replaced by high-rise public housing units. Area residents also indicated that any new housing built in Trefann should not look like modern suburban housing; they preferred it to look like the existing housing. Even the planner's attempts to introduce more open spaces around the new housing was rejected by the people of Trefann. Such spaces might be popular in suburban developments but Trefann residents viewed them as potential nuisances that would become congregating places for local teenagers.

By May 1971 the first phase of the urban renewal plan was drawn up by Howard Cohen and approved by the working committee. It incorporated many of the ideas of the area's residents. "The basic approach," wrote Cohen in his description of the plan, "will be to maintain and reinforce the inherent strengths and perform such remedial work as is necessary, while retaining the indigenous nature of Trefann Court." In keeping with this approach, the first phase of renewal called for the acquisition of the three auto-wrecking plants, the demolition of ten badly run-down houses, and the building of new two- and three-storey row housing. Some of the new houses were to contain apartments, while others were to be for single families.

The first phase was approved by the city in June 1971 and then forwarded to the provincial and federal governments for similar approval. No work could be undertaken until both these levels of government approved the plan and released the money necessary to implement it. By December 1971 the necessary approval came from the provincial and federal governments.

In the meantime, work was almost completed on the whole plan for the Trefann area. Basically, it incorporated the same ideas as were contained in the first-phase plan. Wherever possible, the older homes were to be rehabilitated with urban renewal money. Loans were to be made available to homeowners so that they could make basic repairs to their properties and those who wished to undertake additional renovation work were to be eligible for grants. New housing, where it was built, was to be row housing that would blend in with the area's existing housing.

The final plan for Trefann was not restricted to outlining physical details only. Equal weight was given to the need for social planning in the area. In drawing up the plan, both Howard Cohen and the members of the working committee were concerned not only with *where* people lived but also *how* people lived. They recognized that the Trefann area contained many single parents, old people, and people on welfare, whose problems would not be solved through the physical replanning of the neighborhood. To help these people, the final plan contained a suggestion that the city establish a community council and hire two community workers to deal with matters of importance to the community aside from urban renewal. Although the working committee did not have the power to develop social plans for the area, the importance of this planning aspect was clearly spelled out in the final plan's document: ". . . there must be a social approach," the document stated, "because without it urban renewal will change only the physical setting in which people live. It is the quality of life in the area which must be improved with increased opportunities for personal development and achievement."

The document detailing the urban renewal plan for the Trefann area, officially titled the Trefann Court Urban Renewal Scheme, was 120 pages long. It represented long hours of work put in by members of the working committee and Howard Cohen. When it was presented to city council for approval in January 1972, the visitors' gallery was filled with Trefann area residents, all anxiously awaiting the official reaction to the plan. They were extremely happy when the council members showed general agreement with the plan's recommendations concerning the type of physical renewal that should take place in the area.

Once this had been approved, however, a lengthy debate took place over the question of how the plan was to be implemented. The working committee members had discussed this question at great length while preparing the final document. They were aware that the city, assuming it approved the plan, would need to hire a number of officials to attend to all the physical details, such as making official zoning changes, raising money, and so on, that were necessary to put the plan into practice. It was extremely important to the working committee that anyone hired by the city to work on any aspect of urban renewal in Trefann be sympathetic to the aims and objectives of the plan. Thus the working committee submitted to city council, along with the final document, a motion requesting the city to allow the working committee to participate in the hiring of any officials who would be involved in implementing the plan. This request was, in the opinion of the working committee, a reasonable one. After all, they had participated in the hiring of a planner to draw up the plan.

The initial reaction of the city was to reject the request. Various aldermen argued that to accept it would give too much power to the working committee. After a lengthy debate, during which it became clear that the city would lose the support of the working committee unless the request was granted, city council voted in its favor. At the same time a number of aldermen stressed the fact that the ultimate responsibility, both for carrying out the urban renewal plan and for hiring the necessary staff, resided with city council. The power of the working committee was definitely restricted to the making of recommendations that could be accepted or rejected by the city. "It has to be very clear at the outset," commented one alderman, "as we go into this Trefann urban renewal scheme, that this is a scheme of the City of Toronto and not of the working committee; this is financed by government and not by the working committee; the employees are employees of this government . . . and not of the working committee; and they are hired and sometimes dismissed by this council and not by the working committee . . . the working committee is an advisory committee."

Implementing the Working Committee's Plan

Federal and provincial government approval of the plan was acquired by late 1972. The actual implementation of the plan, however, proved to be extremely difficult. Financial problems surrounded it. The federal and provincial governments refused to release urban renewal money for the rehabilitation of old homes—an essential part of the plan. There was, the two levels of government maintained, no source of money available for this purpose. When it appeared that nothing could be done, the city decided that it would release funds to finance improvements on old homes.

Other financial problems related to the building of new houses in the area. Originally the plan called for 26 such houses to be built, but the federal government would only finance 17. By the summer of 1974 these houses were completed, but it was not until 29 December 1975 that the first occupant moved in. The 18-month delay between the completion of the houses and their occupancy was caused by arguments between the working committee and the federal government over how the new houses were to be sold.

It had been agreed by both the working committee and the federal government that while eight of the new houses would be rented, the remaining nine would be sold to working-class people. Trefann area residents were also to have the first chance to buy or rent the houses. In order to offer the houses for sale at a price that working-class people could afford, the working committee wanted the federal government to lease the land under each house to the buyer at a very low cost. In this way the buyer would only pay for the actual house, thus reducing the total purchase price by $15 000 to $20 000. To prevent people from buying the houses at reduced prices and then reselling them for large profits, the working committee also wanted certain re-sale restrictions placed on the homeowners. These restrictions would not allow the owners to sell their homes for any profit they could get but only for the original price they had paid, plus any amount by which prices had risen in Toronto since the time they had purchased their properties. In other words, if prices had risen 10 percent during this time, the homeowners would be entitled to make a 10-percent profit on the intial purchase price when they sold their properties. By insisting on this resale provision, the working committee hoped to keep the price of the homes low enough that other working-class people would be able to buy the homes when the original owners wanted to sell them.

The federal government objected to the provisions both for selling and reselling the houses. Federal officials argued that, as public funds had been used to build the houses, potential buyers should pay for both the houses and the land and that alternative resale restrictions should be placed on owners who later wished to sell their homes. Allowing homeowners an increase in the value of their homes equivalent to general price increases was, according to one such official, a "blatant get-rich scheme at the taxpayers' expense." Instead, the federal government offered to allow people to buy the homes under the Assisted Home Ownership Program (AHOP). This special federal program was designed to help people with low incomes to buy homes by reducing down payments and by providing grants and repayable monthly loans to subsidize a family's carrying charges. The grants and the mortgage subsidies were repayable after five years. Under this scheme the resale price of the homes was controlled for five years, after which homeowners could sell at any price they could get. No one on the working committee was satisfied with the AHOP provisions, which, by not allowing the land to be leased at reduced cost, would drive prices beyond the means of most Trefann people. Furthermore, by placing no resale restrictions on owners who sold after five years, the working committee felt that in time only middle-class people would be able to afford them. For these reasons, the federal government's AHOP was refused.

While the working committee and the federal government continued to debate how the new houses were to be sold, Trefann residents who hoped to purchase or rent the homes were getting angrier and angrier. Most of these people were living in substandard accommodation and were anxious to move into the new homes that had been sitting empty for so long. But no one could move until the selling details had been resolved. Members of the working committee were accused of demanding too much from the federal government and were urged to seek a settlement. As the pressure to resolve the conflict increased, the working committee eventually and reluctantly withdrew their sale and resale provisions and accepted an alternative arrangement to the AHOP that was offered by the federal government.

Under this arrangement buyers could purchase the houses at a specially subsidized cost set by the government. The land was to be leased to homeowners for $57 a year and down payments were to be $1500. Future resale prices were to vary only slightly from the original price. Owners who wished to sell were entitled to receive as profit an increase (equal to the amount prices had risen in Toronto) on the down payment and on the small amount of principal in the monthly mortgage payment. So, if prices rose 10 percent, such owners would receive a 10-percent profit only on the $1500 down payment and on whatever amount of principal they had repaid. The working committee argued that homeowners who bought under this arrangement would have all the responsibilities of home ownership in terms of upkeep of their properties, but few of the privileges in terms of making a reasonable profit when they sold. However, after 18 months of argument the working committee gave in.

Within weeks the houses were occupied. Prices ranged from \$21 000 to \$29 000, considerably less than equivalent homes were selling for throughout Toronto at that time. Toronto, like most Canadian cities, had witnessed a sharp increase in home prices during the time that the Trefann Court Urban Renewal Scheme was slowly being implemented. Although the new homes were sold at a price that some Trefann residents could afford, other older homes in the area had increased in value at a phenomenal rate. While this resulted in part from the general increase in house prices throughout the city, another reason stemmed from a rapidly developing attraction for the Trefann area on the part of the middle class. Ironically, the attempts to improve the area for working-class people seemed to have backfired. The improvements brought about through the efforts of the working committee caused some middle-class individuals to look for housing there. It became a new "in" area in which to live. Real estate advertisements describing Trefann as "a townhouse potential area" and "the heart of the townhouse redevelopment area" offered "Victorian townhouses" for \$80 000 and up. Many working-class homeowners, who had actively participated in planning urban renewal in Trefann, could not resist selling their homes at large profits. When they did so, the middle class moved in.

By early 1976, when the 17 new houses were finally occupied, Trefann Court was no longer the solidly working-class area that it had been when its residents first decided to fight the city's plans for urban renewal. Despite what had been described as a "breakthrough" in urban planning—the creation of a system that allowed city officials to work with area representatives in planning their neighborhood—few people were happy with the results. "In terms of its concept as a decent environment for low-income people," commented one City Hall official who had been closely associated with the plan and its implementation, "Trefann Court is a failure."

The Issues IV

Given the variety of interests and needs involved, was the urban renewal plan that was eventually adopted for Trefann Court (i.e., the mixed residential and industrial nature was to be retained through the demolition of some houses and industries, the rehabilitation of other houses, and the construction of some new ones) the best compromise solution?

Urban Renewal

A. Selection

- Do you agree with the comment that because the surrounding areas had undergone urban renewal, leaving Trefann Court as the last remaining eyesore in Cabbagetown, some sort of renewal had to take place there?
- One commentator wrote that the major reason for selecting Trefann Court as an urban renewal area was that it looked "ugly" and that because it was a small compact area, urban renewal would be easy. In your opinion, is this a factor in favor of urban renewal in Trefann Court or in any other area?
- Some people oppose the development of high-rise residential buildings because they consider them to be "ugly." Is this a factor in favor of tearing them down? Does the fact that high-rises are a relatively cheap and efficient way of housing people outweigh the fact that they are not as attractive as single-family homes?
- Did the fact that most of the homes in the Trefann area were old and difficult to maintain help to justify the city's original plan to tear them down?
- Given what you know about the conditions existing

in Trefann Court do you agree with the city's decision in selecting the area for urban renewal? If so, how would you have gone about deciding the kind of renewal most appropriate for the area?

Parallel Situation

The Ontario provincial government's decision to close Toronto's Don Jail met with the approval of most Toronto residents. The 115-year-old building had long been criticized for its lack of proper facilities and its outmoded and inadequate safety provisions. No one was sorry when the last inmates of the jail were transferred to more modern prisons. Shortly thereafter, however, the fate of the old institution became the centre of a fierce debate when the government announced plans for demolishing the building and turning the site into a park. According to Ontario's Minister of Corrections, Frank Drea, there were too many unpleasant memories associated with the jail, including the suicide of many prisoners and the hanging of prisoners found guilty of murder, for it to be left standing.

Support for the government's plans came from various people who agreed that the jail represented a "monument to misery" and, as such, must be torn down. There were, however, a number of groups and individuals, including a majority of the members of Toronto's City Council, who felt that the building should be saved and an alternative use found for it. They argued that, despite its associations, the jail should be kept because it represented a classic example of Italian Renaissance architecture that was both beautiful and unique. While petitions were presented to the government seeking the building's preservation, Toronto City Council sought suggestions from the public on alternative uses. Suggestions varied from turning it into a museum to using it as new headquarters for the Toronto Humane Society. Appeals to private developers to buy the building met with no success, especially when it was estimated that it would cost approximately seven million dollars to purchase it and a further two-and-a-half million dollars to convert it. So, to the relief of some and the dismay of others, it seemed inevitable that the Don Jail would soon be replaced by a park.

• Should the Don Jail be torn down because
 -it is 115 years old and needs modernizing?
 -there are unpleasant memories associated with its use?

• If there were pleasant memories associated with it (e.g., it had been used as a famous art museum), would you want to see it demolished?

Given that the building has architectural merit, should it be saved? Should the provincial government provide the money for conversion?

• Would you recommend that the Don Jail be preserved and converted for use as any of the following
 -an apartment building for "undesirables"?
 -a home for the aged?
 -an apartment building for low-income people?
 -a luxury condominium apartment building?
 -a treatment centre for alcoholics?
 -a place of worship?
 -a school?

• In what way is the decision to demolish the Don Jail similar to the original decision to tear down most of the homes in Trefann Court?

B. Effects – Compensation

• Even before the city approved its original renewal plan for Trefann, did it have a responsibility to ensure that housing standards did not deteriorate in the area?

• What responsibility did the city have to find similar rented accommodation in the same or a similar area for the tenants who lived in Trefann Court?

- Under the circumstances should the city have agreed to pay moving costs for any residents who had to vacate their homes in Trefann Court?
- Should the city have agreed to pay homeowners "replacement value" for their homes rather than "market value." Why? Why not?
- Would it make any difference if a businessman rather than the city had wanted to buy the homes in order to replace them with a private development?
- When the city and the homeowners were unable to agree on a fair price for the homes should the city have continued to negotiate or should it have expropriated the homes and paid the owners the original amount that had been offered to them?
- What price should the city have been willing to pay for the homes
  - -the market value?
  - -the minimum amount it could get away with?
  - -all costs involved in relocating people to equivalent homes, including replacement value and moving costs?
- Since the fact that the city had plans to carry out urban renewal in Trefann Court directly influenced the lowering of house values in the area, is it fair that the city should profit from a situation of its own making at the expense of the homeowners?

C. Demolition vs. Rehabilitation

- The Federal Task Force on Housing and Urban Development recommended that instead of the traditional method of urban renewal, involving the tearing down of old houses, local authorities should encourage the upgrading of older homes in run-down sections of the community. Do you agree with this recommendation? Why? Why not?

- In an area like Trefann Court, what advantages/disadvantages were to be gained from
    - -demolishing the old homes and replacing them with new ones?
    - -rehabilitating the old homes?
- Should public grants be given to Trefann homeowners to improve their properties? Why? Why not?
- In each of the following situations should the homeowners be eligible for a public grant? If so, should there be a means test to determine the homeowner's eligibility?
    - -Mr. White, a wealthy lawyer, buys a large, old home that is of historic interest but badly in need of repair. He decides to replace the old kitchen and bathroom and applies to his local authority for a grant to cover the cost.
    - -Mr. and Mrs. Litvick, a retired couple living on an old-age pension, discover that their roof is leaking. They apply to their local authority for a grant to cover the cost of installing a new roof.
    - -Mr. and Mrs. Schmidt find their home cramped with two adults and six children living there. As they cannot afford a larger house, they decide to add another room to their present home and they apply to their local authority for a grant to cover the cost.
- What obligation does a government have to maintain existing houses or to provide appropriate housing for its citizens?
- If homeowners receive improvement grants that increase the value of their homes, and then sell their homes, should they be allowed to keep any profit they make? Should such profits revert to the local authority from whom they received the grant or should they have to repay the grant if they decide to sell their homes?

Citizen Participation

- Did the residents of Trefann Court have a right to be

consulted about the planned changes for their community?

• In most cases would a residents group's unanimous support for, or rejection of, a plan be sufficient reason for its approval or rejection by a local authority?

• When the two resident associations (TCRA and TNT) were unable to agree on their objectives for urban renewal, should the city have drawn up its own plan for the area? Should it have had the right to ignore both associations' wishes or would it have been obliged to draft a compromise plan?

• Planning is a lengthy process that requires a considerable amount of professional expertise. What advantages/disadvantages are there in involving ordinary citizens in this process?

• Who should be involved in the planning process for a neighborhood

-neighborhood property owners?
-neighborhood tenants?
-elected municipal politicians?
-municipal planners?
-any other individual or group?

• Should the working committee have been involved in selecting a planner to draw up the scheme for renewal in Trefann Court?

• Should the working committee alone have selected the planner?

• When Toronto City Council voted in favor of the working committee's scheme for urban renewal in Trefann one alderman commented, ". . . this is a scheme of the City of Toronto and not of the working committee; this is financed by government and not by the working committee; the employees are employees of this government . . . and not of the working committee; and they are hired and sometimes dismissed by this council and not by the working committee . . . the working committee is an advisory committee."

- -Do you agree with these comments concerning the power of the working committee?
- -What involvement do you think the committee should have had in implementing the Trefann Court urban renewal scheme?

• Given the fact that they are not elected publicly, what powers should citizen groups have?

Neighborhood Composition

• The proposals for the Trefann area drawn up by the residents were designed to retain the working-class nature of the community. Is it legitimate for residents to encourage only certain kinds of people to live in their area in order to retain its nature? Should they determine what kind of people should live in their area?

• Would you agree to a local community group encouraging the kind of people that can live in its area so that it will comprise only

- -very poor people?
- -very rich people?
- -West Indians?
- -Europeans?
- -Muslims?
- -Christians?
- -Jews?

• Should everyone have the right to choose where they will live as long as they can afford to do so?

Parallel Situation

Until the late 1960s the Don Vale area of Toronto was an important source of inexpensive housing for low-income people. Then middle-class professionals, attracted by the Victorian charm of the nineteenth-century houses to be found there and the close location of the area to the city centre, began moving in. Many of the houses they bought were rooming houses and once the owner sold the property, the tenants were forced out and had great problems finding similar inexpensive accommodation. As more and more of these former rooming houses were renovated into fashionable townhouses, some of the new owners became concerned about the tenants' plight. They decided to apply to the federal government for money to purchase and renovate a group of 33 houses in the area. Their plan was to convert the houses into apartments to provide low-cost, subsidized accommodation for people who were being forced out of the area as a result of the influx of the middle classes.

This plan met with considerable hostility from many of the area's middle-class residents, who felt it would cause a drop in local property values. When money was granted to proceed with the project, angry homeowners organized protest meetings and wrote numerous letters to the local newspapers defending their right to decide who should live in the area. "Why must we be made to feel guilty for wanting our area, with our friends and our children's friends across the street?" asked one of these residents. Another summed up their feelings by asking, "Why do we have to justify our desire and our need and our rights to live in a cohesive community where we will find people like us?" Despite these protests, however, the project was completed.

• Were the homeowners justified in opposing the plan for low-income housing in their area?

• What advantages/disadvantages are there to having people with differing incomes and from differing social classes living in the same area?

• In order to maintain a supply of suitable accommodation for low-income people, should local authorities place restrictions of the sale of properties normally occupied by such people? Should high-income people be kept out of certain areas because their purchasing of homes there would drive up prices and force low-income people to move out?

- If property values were to drop in Don Vale because of the low-income housing project, should homeowners receive financial compensation to cover their losses? If so, should this compensation be provided by
  - the federal government because it granted the money for the low-income housing project?
  - the local authority because it approved the plans for the project?
  - the group of homeowners who originally drew up the plans for the project?
- Are both the Don Vale residents and the Trefann Court residents *equally* justified in wanting to restrict the kind of people who will live in their neighborhoods? Does one group have a stronger case than the other? If so, for what reasons?

Social Planning

- The final plan for Trefann Court suggested that the city should be responsible for social planning, or *how* the areas' residents lived, in addition to the physical planning of where they lived. Do you agree that the local authority should be responsible for social planning? Should it provide community facilities to help single parents, old people, people on welfare, and families facing various kinds of problems? Should it provide parks and entertainment facilities?
- Should local authorities have a right to redesign a neighborhood and move people out if it
  - becomes so run-down that it is a health hazard?
  - suffers too many robberies?
  - is overrun by pornographic book stores and movie houses?

- Should social planning for an area be done by
  - -residents who live in the area?
  - -experts in social planning in consultation with the area's residents?
  - -experts responsible for overall social planning throughout a local authority's jurisdiction?

The New Houses

- Given the fact that the new houses in Trefann Court were built with federal money and were designed to accommodate low-income people, should the selling price have been subsidized?
- According to federal officials, if no resale restrictions were placed on the houses this would result in a "blatant get-rich scheme at the taxpayers expense." Do you agree? How long should the resale restrictions be applied to the new homes in Trefann? Why?
- Is it right that homes purchased under a government subsidy program should have *all* resale restrictions lifted after a certain period of time? Should not *some* resale restrictions be made permanent so that other low-income families may purchase affordable homes whenever they are available for sale? If so, what kind of permanent resale restrictions would you recommend? If not, why not?
- Should only subsidized homeowners be subjected to resale restrictions or should the profit any homeowner makes through selling a house be restricted? If so, how and whose responsibility should it be to control resale profits? If not, why not?

Home Ownership Subsidy Programs

During the 1970s many low income families were encouraged to buy homes because of the availability of various federal government schemes providing mortgage subsidies. Most of these subsidies were available for five years on the assumption that by this time the low-income homeowner would be able to pay the full mortgage rates on their homes. However, in late 1979 and early 1980, these homeowners faced a crisis situation upon the expiry of the government subsidy program when they found that mortgage rates had risen to an unprecedented high of 15 percent. Under the mortgage subsidy programs most of these homeowners had been paying around 8 percent and the record high new rates meant an 80% increase in monthly carrying charges. Faced with such an increase, a number of homeowners who were unable to keep up the payments on their homes were forced to sell them if they could find buyers and, in some cases, where no buyers could be found, homes were abandoned. Angry homeowners pleaded for government action to help them pay their mortgages but proposals aimed at assisting people caught in a financial squeeze were shelved when mortgage rates began to drop.

• Did the federal government have a responsibility to assist homeowners who had purchased homes under a subsidy program and who were in danger of losing them because of the increase in mortgage rates? What kind of assistance would you recommend? Why?

• Should homeowners who lost their homes because they were unable to pay the higher mortgage rates once the subsidies were withdrawn receive financial compensation from the government for any losses they incurred? Why? Why not?

• Should government programs aimed at helping low-income families purchase a home contain provisions for the continued subsidization of monthly carrying charges if homeowners are unable to make such payments once the original subsidy period expires?

• Should the government have a permanent mortgage subsidy program designed to help *any* homeowner faced with the threat of losing a home because of increased mortgage rates? If so, what kind of program would you design?

The Island Homes

A five-minute ferry ride from downtown Toronto brings you to a group of small islands known as the Toronto Islands. In addition to a number of fine beaches, the Islands consist of many acres of well-kept parkland, picnic areas, children's play areas, and camping sites. No private cars are allowed on these Islands, so people move around on foot or by bicycle. For almost 100 years the Toronto Islands have been a major recreational site for the residents of Toronto and its surrounding areas.

During the late 1890s a number of wealthy Toronto residents began leasing Island land from the City of Toronto, which officially owned all the Islands. On this leased land large summer homes were erected. For almost half a century these were the only homes on the Islands. By the mid-1940s, however, most of these homes had been demolished and replaced by an even larger number of more modest year-round homes. The building of these houses was encouraged by the City of Toronto to meet the severe housing crisis that faced the city at the end of World War II. War veterans and their families were granted land leases and building subsidies by the city. At no time, however, did the amount of land used for either the large summer homes or the more modest war veterans' homes occupy very much of the Islands' overall space. Most of this space continued to be public parkland maintained by the city for recreational purposes.

In 1953 the City of Toronto was amalgamated with its surrounding boroughs to form Metropolitan Toronto (Metro) and, at that time, ownership of the Toronto

Islands and the leases on the Island homes passed from the city to Metro. Two years later Metro announced plans to demolish all the houses on the Islands and to return the entire area to parkland. During the following twelve years many of the homes, in poor repair, were found to be unsafe by municipal building inspectors and were torn down, forcing residents to leave the Islands. Also, leases that terminated during this period were generally not renewed. Continual inspection and harassment, plus the insecurity of lease renewal, caused many long-standing Island residents to pack up and leave. Once they did, their homes were levelled without delay. There was no financial compensation for the residents when their homes were torn down. Some, who left before they were forced out, did not try to sell their homes; the houses had no commercial value and few people were interested in investing in them when the future was so insecure. In the few cases where the homes were sold, they went for a token amount, generally little more than a few thousand dollars.

By 1968, 600 Island homes had been demolished, leaving about 700 people living on the Toronto Islands in two communities consisting of a total of 250 homes. Over the years these people had watched their friends and neighbors leave as their houses had been torn down. Of those who remained, many were the original war veteran settlers and their families and some were relative newcomers who had bought homes there despite the insecurity as to how long Metro would allow these homes to remain. Faced with the common threat of losing their homes, the remaining residents decided to seek legal advice in order to prevent Metro from tearing down any more of their homes. Lawyers were hired who, from 1968 to 1973, successfully fought Metro's attempts to terminate any more leases. Encouraged by this success, the Island residents became convinced that Metro would eventually give up its plans to demolish their homes.

After all, they argued, these homes occupied only 5 percent or 27 acres [about 11 hectares] of the Toronto Islands' land area, leaving 625 acres [about 253 hectares] of open space for public park use. But the residents' short period of security was abruptly shattered in 1973 when Metro served all the Island residents with one year's notice to vacate their homes. At the same time Metro announced that the 27 acres [about 11 hectares] occupied by the Island homes would be used to build a public ice rink, swimming pool, and a campsite for underprivileged children.

Although dismayed by the event, the Island residents immediately decided to challenge Metro's action in the courts. By claiming that the wording on the notices they had received was unclear, they were successful in obtaining extensions on their leases until 1975. With this victory in hand, the residents then petitioned the Ontario Court of Appeal to rule that the notices were totally invalid because of the unclear wording. The Ontario Court of Appeal agreed with the residents and ruled in their favor. Metro, however, refused to give up its attempts to clear the Island homes and proceeded to challenge the Court of Appeal's ruling in the Supreme Court of Canada.

While the case was before the Supreme Court, both sides tried to convince the public that their opposing positions on the issue were correct. The Islanders argued that of the existing 625 acres [about 253 hectares] of public parkland on the Islands, many large areas were hardly ever used by the public even during busy summer months. These areas, they claimed, could easily be used by Metro to build an ice rink, swimming pool, and a camp for underprivileged children. Spokesmen for the residents also argued that by tearing down the Island homes Metro would only succeed in adding to the severe housing crisis that already existed in Metro, as few of the displaced homeowners could afford to buy or rent equivalent homes on the mainland. And those Islanders who could afford to live in the city simply did not want to do so. "I like the smaller community here and I don't want to live in the city," one resident told a reporter. Another admitted to the same reporter that she didn't want to move because it would be impossible to reproduce such "an idyllic existence amidst parkland" anywhere in the city.

This "idyllic existence" of the Island residents was used by Metro as an argument in its favor. The Islands, they claimed, belonged to all taxpayers and hence it was unfair that a "small group of taxpayers" should enjoy the "unique privilege" of living there all year round. Taxpayers' money was used to maintain the Islands for public use, not for private homeowners. Furthermore, Metro suggested that many of these homeowners were, in fact, "well heeled and professional people" who would have no problems finding alternative accommodation.

As the arguments on both sides continued, the Island residents brought another legal suit against Metro on the grounds of discrimination, when three private yacht clubs located on the Islands were each given ten-year extended leases and promises of increased land. Why, the residents wanted to know, were private yacht clubs allowed to remain on the Islands that Metro insisted were "public recreation property?" The judge hearing the case responded by stating that yachting clubs were valid recreational facilities to be using public lands and the Islanders lost their suit.

In June 1977 the Islanders lost again when the Supreme Court of Canada ruled six to three that Metro's original notices were valid and that homeowners would have to vacate. Their initial shock and profound depression at the decision quickly gave way to a renewed determination to continue the fight against Metro. The Islanders were supported by members of Toronto City Council who announced that they would refuse to grant

Metro the demolition permits needed to tear down the houses. Further support was promised by Larry Grossman, the provincial member of parliament in whose constituency the Island residents lived. The provincial legislature, he assured the residents, would be sympathetic to their cause "because it's sympathetic to housing and you don't tear down homes in the midst of a housing crisis." But while the Islanders gathered support for their cause, Metro announced that it would fight any further attempts to delay the four-year-old battle to evict the remaining homeowners.

For over two years Metro Council opposed all attempts to delay the eviction of the remaining homeowners and, finally, in 1979 it voted to evict the Islanders by July 1980. Toronto City Council responded by voting in April 1980 to buy back part of the Toronto Islands from Metro. The city offered to pay Metro $750 000 for part of the Toronto Islands, including the land occupied by the 250 remaining houses. Of these, only those that could be repaired or renovated to meet the city's bylaw on housing standards were to be retained, and their occupants were to receive new land leases from the city. The city's plan also called for the building of up to 250 new housing units on the land they sought to purchase. One-third of the housing was to be available for private ownership on land leased from the city at market value, while the rest was to be allocated for non-profit or co-operative housing. But hope that the city's offer would be approved by Metro Council was very slim. While awaiting Metro's response, the provincial government announced that it would introduce a bill into the legislature designed to help the Island residents. Under this bill, the present occupants would be permitted to remain in their homes until they died, but no longer, and owners would be forbidden to sell or lease their houses. When homes became vacant through death or for other reasons, the government bill called for tearing them down and turning the land back into parkland. Opposition parties in the legislature vowed to combine to defeat the bill, claiming that it would fail to preserve the Island community. Island residents were equally opposed to the legislation, which they described as guaranteed to bring about "the death by inches" of their community.

The Issues

Should the Island Homes be demolished?

Rights and Privileges

• Do the residents of the Island homes have a right to continue living there because

- there has been a long tradition of homes located in Toronto Islands?
- the city encouraged the development of housing there to ease the housing shortage after World War II?
- the land occupied by the homes is only 5 percent of the Islands total land area?

If so, do the residents have this right indefinitely?

• Given that the Island homeowners enjoy the benefits of living in a particularly attractive environment, should the privilege of living there be available to everyone? Should the residents pay more than the regular real estate taxes because of their privileged existence?

• Should people who live next to any large public park pay higher real estate taxes and/or have to contribute towards the maintenance of the park?

• Should Metro agree to sell the 27 acres [about 11 hectares] of land occupied by houses to the residents? Why? Why not? If so, should Metro have the right to sell off 5 percent of High Park or Queen's Park, both of which are heavily used city parks?

• Do you agree with the City of Toronto's 1980 plan to buy part of the Toronto Islands in order to (a) lease the land to the Island residents (b) build new private and public housing? Why? Why not?

• Does the fact that the Toronto Islands are public land owned by Metro Toronto give it the absolute right to decide how such land is to be used? Should Metro have the right to expropriate private land for a public park if it thinks a park is needed?

• Would you support a decision to tear down the Island homes and replace them with
- -a public works yard?
- -a housing development for low-income people?
- -an entertainment complex consisting of a concert hall, a theatre, and a couple of movie houses?
- -a short take-off and landing (STOL) airport?

• Should any local authority have the right to expropriate land
- -for a public utility?
- -for defense needs?
- -for a second airport?
- -for a land bank? (Land banking involves the purchase of land when the price is cheap in order to keep down prices at a later date.)
- -owned by foreigners if the rates of foreign-owned land exceed the rates of domestic-owned land?

• Is Metro justified in continuing to lease land on the Toronto Islands to private yacht clubs? Was Metro justified in extending the leases of these clubs while terminating the leases on the Island homes? Would it make any difference if only public rather than private yacht clubs were allowed to lease Island land?

The Homes

• Should the fact that the Island residents like living in a small community and do not want to relocate in the city be an important consideration in making a decision as to whether or not the homes will be torn down?

• Do you agree with Metro that the homes should be demolished because the residents are enjoying an "idyllic" existence at the taxpayer's expense? Is it really at the taxpayer's expense? Why? Why not? Is it right to tear down the homes because only a few people can live there rather than everyone?

• Should the fact that there is a shortage of moderately priced housing influence Metro's decision to demolish the Island homes? Would it make any difference if (a) all, (b) a majority, or (c) a minority of the Island residents could afford to buy homes elsewhere?

• Do you support the provincial government's proposals for allowing the Island residents to remain in their homes until they die or move and then to tear down the houses? Why? Why not?

• Should houses ever be torn down to provide recreational space? Would it make any difference if the houses were

-worth a lot of money?
-worth very little money?
-in good condition?
-in poor condition?

BIBLIOGRAPHY

General

Axworthy, Lloyd, and Gillies, James M. *The City: Canada's Prospects Canada's Problems.* Toronto: Butterworth and Co., 1973.

Berry, Brian J. L. *The Human Consequences of Urbanization.* London: Macmillan, 1974.

Bryfogle, R. Charles, and Krueger, Ralph R., eds. *Urban Problems.* Rev. ed. Toronto: Holt, Rinehart and Winston, 1975.

Gertler, Leonard O. *Urban Issues.* Toronto: Van Nostrand Reinhold, 1976.

Higgins, Donald J. H. *Urban Canada: Its Government and Politics.* Toronto: Macmillan, 1977.

Jacobs, Jane. *The Death and Life of Great American Cities.* New York: Vintage Books, 1961.

Powell, Alan, ed. *The City: Attacking Modern Myths.* Toronto: McClelland and Stewart, 1974.

Rutherford, Paul, ed. *Saving the Canadian City: The First Phase 1880–1920: An Anthology of Earlier Articles on Urban Reform.* Toronto: University of Toronto Press, 1974.

Simmons, James, and Simmons, Robert. *Urban Canada.* 2d ed. Toronto: Copp Clark, 1974.

Weaver, John C. *Shaping the Canadian City: Essays on Urban Politics and Policy, 1890-1920.* Toronto: Institute of Public Administration of Canada, 1977.

Transportation

Budden, Sandra, and Ernst, Joseph. *The Movable Airport.* Toronto: Hakkert, 1973.

Metropolitan Toronto Transportation Plan Review. *Choices for the Future.* Summary Report, no. 64. Toronto: Metropolitan Toronto, 1975.

Nowlan, David, and Nowlan, Nadine. *The Bad Trip.* Toronto: New Press, 1970.

Owen, Wilfred. *The Accessible City.* Washington, D.C.: Brookings Institution, 1972.

Urban Renewal and Community Action

Fraser, Graham. *Fighting Back.* Toronto: Hakkert, 1972.

Granatstein, J. L. *Marlborough Marathon.* Toronto: Hakkert and James Lewis and Samuel, 1971.

Keating, Donald R. *The Power to Make It Happen.* Toronto: Green Tree, 1975.

Lorimer, James. *The Real World of City Politics.* Toronto: James Lewis and Samuel, 1970.

Pasternak, Jack. *The Kitchener Market Fight.* Toronto: Samuel Stevens and Hakkert, 1975.

Sewell, John. *Up against City Hall.* Toronto: James Lewis and Samuel, 1972.

Pollution

Addison, William. *People and Pollution.* Toronto: Gage Educational, 1977.

Bates, David V. *A Citizen's Guide to Air Pollution.* Montreal: McGill/Queen's University Press, 1972.

Nadler, Allen et al. *Air Pollution.* New York: Scientists' Institute for Public Information, 1970.

Rounthwaite, Ann. *Pollution and the Law in Canada.* Vancouver: International Self-Counsel Press, 1975.

Periodicals

City Magazine. Published by The Charlottetown Group Publishing Inc., 35 Britain Street, Toronto, Ontario M5A 1R7.

Urban Forum. Published by the Canadian Council on Urban and Regional Research, 251 Laurier West, Suite 1100, Ottawa, Ontario K1P 5J6.

Games and Kits

Ferguson, J. *Air Pollution.* Scarborough, Ont.: McGraw Hill, 1971. A resource kit for class examination of the cause, effect, and possible solution to air pollution in three major cities: Toronto, Vancouver, and Pittsburgh.

Simpolis. Cambridge, Mass.: Abt Associates, 1970. A simulation game that presents a dramatic encounter with seven major urban problem areas of transportation, education, housing, civil rights, poverty, crime, and pollution.

The Schools Council/Nuffield Humanities Project. *Living in Cities.* London: Heinemann, 1973. A collection of records, slides, articles, filmstrips, cartoons, stories, booklets, etc. Comes with teacher's manual.

Vogel, Rex. *Metro Government: A Simulation Game.* Edmonton: Canadian Social Sciences Services, 1972. A set of five simulation games designed to show how an alderman works. Each game teaches some aspects of the workings of a city government.

Films

General

A Future for the Past. Color. 30 mins. Focusses on city planning, concentrating on preserving historical landmarks and integrating new buildings with old ones in order to preserve the character of an area. Available from Visual Education Centre, 75 Horner Avenue, Unit 1, Toronto, Ontario M8Z 4X5.

*A Town Meeting on Cities and Suburbs: Centres or

Spread City? Color. 59 mins. Explores the advantages and problems associated with two urban issues, namely, rebuilding the downtown area of older cities or building on open land outside cities. Available from Marlin Motion Pictures, 47 Lakeshore Road East, Port Credit, Ontario L5G 1C9.

City Limits. Color. 28 mins. NFB. A film essay in which Jane Jacobs analyses the problems that plague all big cities and suggests that creative solutions can come from ordinary citizens interested in saving their communities and their environment.

City under Pressure. B&W. 18 mins. NFB. A case study of Edmonton, dealing with local government and the pressure that groups can apply to city planning. Considers such problems as the optimum use of public land.

Metro Toronto a municipal partnership. Color. 25 mins. Traces historically the merger of city and suburbs into what is known today as Metropolitan Toronto. Available from Metro Toronto Planning Board, City Hall, Toronto, Ontario M5H 2N1.

The City and Its Region. B&W. 28 mins. NFB. This film shows how cities thrive best when they live in harmony and balance with the countryside and explores how this balance can be maintained or restored in today's sprawling metropolitan regions.

Housing

A Town Meeting on Housing: A Place to Live. Color. 59 mins. Looks at the housing situation in the New York region where the housing shortage, together with the high taxes and rents on existing homes, makes it virtually impossible for people to live where they want to. Viewers are asked to vote on questions trying to resolve the housing problem. Available from Marlin Motion Pictures, 47 Lakeshore Road East, Port Credit, Ontario L5G 1C9.

Where We Live. Color. 20 mins. An edited version of a feature-length film in which Canada's housing problems are examined together with the new answers proposed by town planners. Available from CTV Television Network, 42 Charles Street East, Toronto, Ontario M4Y 1T5.

Pollution

A Town Meeting on Environment: How Fine a Place. Color. 59 mins. Looks at how the New York region has to come to grips with the problems of population, pollution, and parks to provide a decent place to live. Viewers are asked to vote on questions for improving their environment. Available from Marlin Motion Pictures, 47 Lakeshore Road East, Port Credit, Ontario L5G 1C9.

Controversy over Industrial Pollution: A Case Study. Color. 16 mins. The pollution from an aluminum plant in Columbia Falls, Montana, and the effect on plants, animals, and people in the area provide the basis for a discussion of the scientific, social, and economic issues involved. Available from Visual Education Centre, 75 Horner Avenue, Unit 1, Toronto, Ontario M8Z 4X5.

Persistent and Finagling. B&W. 56 mins. NFB. Follows the efforts of members of the Society to Overcome Pollution (STOP) in Montreal as they initiate and direct a project for tackling the pollution problems in their city. It shows the problems encountered by citizens' groups when they try to organize public action.

Pollution Front Line. B&W. 46 mins. NFB. Explores the complexities of the pollution problem in Hamilton, Ontario, from many individual points of view.

The First Mile Up. B&W. 28 mins. NFB. Looks at air pollution as it is encountered in big cities and industrial areas and discusses what is being done and what should be done about it.

Transportation

A Place to Grow (People or Planes). Color. 12 mins. Presents the case of a community opposed to the building of a proposed new airport. Includes the community's suggestions for alternative schemes. Available from

Trickett Productions Ltd., 335 King Street West, Toronto, Ontario M5V 1J5.

A Town Meeting on Transportation: Master or Servant? Color. 59 mins. Looks at the great transportation burden facing the New York region. It is designed to solicit viewers to vote on questions aimed at solving urban transportation problems. Available from Marlin Motion Pictures, 47 Lakeshore Road East, Port Credit, Ontario L5G 1C9.

Cities for People. Color. 25 mins. CBC. "The city is a place for people" is the theme, which describes how unplanned and uncontrolled growth creates disaster for the inhabitants. Leading architects and town planners explain concrete plans for the solution of problems caused by automobiles. Available from Visual Education Centre, 75 Horner Avenue, Unit 1, Toronto, Ontario M8Z 4X5.

The City: Cars or People. B&W. 28 mins. NFB. A study of an old but continuing problem, namely, how to make the city accessible for meeting and mixing without allowing auto transport to make it congested and uninhabitable.

Where Do We Go from Here? Color. 22 mins. NFB. Provides an examination of Toronto's transportation problems and discusses growth and possible future solutions.

OTHER TITLES IN THIS SERIES

Available from General Publishing Co. Ltd.,
30 Lesmill Road, Don Mills, Ontario M3B 2T6:

Don't Teach That! An exploration of areas such as religious education in which teaching in schools touches upon questions of strong personal conviction.

Foreign Ownership. The problems and issues arising from the extensive foreign ownership of business corporations in Canada.

The Law and the Police. Recent cases illustrating the controversy that results when the rights of the individual clash with the process of law enforcement.

Rights of Youth. Situations where conflict arises between the responsibilities of schools and the rights of young people.

Available from Publications Sales, OISE,
252 Bloor Street West, Toronto, Ontario M5S 1V6:

Native Survival. The dilemma of Canada's Indians as the culture and laws of the majority threaten their way of life and their group identity.

Crisis in Quebec. The rise of the Front de Libération du Québec and the events of October 1970 are examined in the political context of Quebec.

On Strike! Several labor-management confrontations of recent years in Canada examined in the light of their impact on workers, business, and the public.

The Right to Live and Die. Case studies around such issues as abortion, sterilization, euthanasia, and capital punishment as they concern the individual, the society, and the law.

Issues in Cultural Diversity. The tensions which often affect relations between minority groups or group members and the wider Canadian community.

Women in Canadian Society. Recent cases on women and work, women and the law, and native women consider claims for equal status with men in these areas.